AMMA:

Inspiring Experiences

with the Divine Mother

AMMA:

Inspiring Experiences

with the Divine Mother

Dayalu (Ted Zeff)

AMMA:
Inspiring Experiences with the Divine Mother

Published by:
Mata Amritanandamayi Center
P.O. Box 613
San Ramon, CA 94583 USA
www.amma.org

Edited by Br. Satish

Address in India:
Mata Amritanandamayi Mission Trust
Amritapuri, Kollam Dt.
Kerala 690546, India
www.amritapuri.org
inform@amritapuri.org

Dedication

This book is dedicated to

the Divine Mother,

Sri Mata Amritanandamayi Devi

("The Sweet Mother of Eternal Bliss").

I humbly bow down at your lotus feet.

Permissions

Acknowledgments

This book could not have been written without the excellent editing skills of Br. Satish. I want to thank Ram Das Batchelder, Avinash Knox, and Teja Watson for giving me innumerable editorial suggestions. I also want to thank especially all the devotees who allowed me to share their amazing and inspirational experiences with Amma. Only through Amma's grace has this book been published. Through her unconditional love for all humanity, Amma continues to inspire me and millions of others to live a more compassionate, balanced, and spiritually uplifting life.

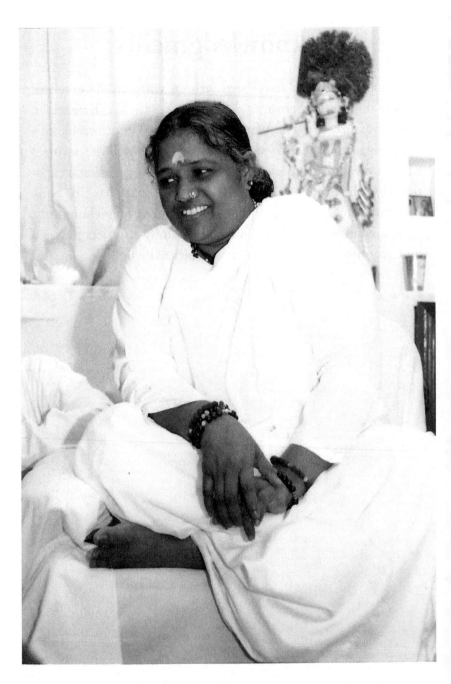

Amma in her room in Amritapuri

Table of Contents

"Everyone in the world should be able to sleep without fear, at least for one night. Everyone should be able to eat to his or her fill, at least for one day. There should be at least one day when hospitals see no one admitted due to violence. By doing selfless service for at least one day, everyone should help the poor and needy. It is Amma's prayer that at least this small dream be realized."

— Amma

Preface

In 1997, I wrote my first book, *Searching For God, Part I*, which included uplifting stories about my experiences (and the experiences of others) with my beloved Guru, Sri Mata Amritanandamayi Devi, from 1988 to 1997. *Searching for God, Part II* included inspiring spiritual experiences from 1997 to 2001. The book you are now reading includes both my and other devotees' experiences with Amma (which means "Mother" in her native language, Malayalam), mostly from 2001 to 2015.

*

This book includes Sanskrit words, which have been italicized the first time they appear in the book and are defined in the glossary.

The answers to the questions in this book that the devotees asked Amma were specific to that particular devotee at that time.

May you become as inspired while reading these experiences with our beloved Divine Mother as I was while collecting and writing them.

Om Amriteshwaryai Namah

Amma giving satsang at the beach in Amritapuri

Introduction

In 1988, when I first met Amma at Fort Mason Center in San Francisco, there were approximately a hundred people who attended the evening program. The following morning, I excitedly arrived early for the morning program that was scheduled to commence at 9:30. When Amma arrived at the small room in an old building south of Market Street in San Francisco, there was only one other person waiting in the room. However, as the morning progressed, Amma slowly blessed about 75 people, and the program ended at around 12:30 p.m.

The crowds were small during Amma's first couple of years in the United States, and no one imagined how huge the programs would soon become. However, since most of the venues were small, it actually felt crowded at most of the sites. I remember being squashed in the small dining room of a Buddhist center in Berkeley with about 60 people slowly moving from all directions toward Amma for *darshan* (audience of a holy person. In Amma's organization, this specifically refers to Amma's embrace).

In the last 25 years, the attendance at Amma's daily programs in the United States has grown from a mere 100 people to up to approximately 6,000 at some programs. In July 2007, during Amma's first visit to Chile, 20,000 people attended one of the evening programs. In India, it is now common to have tens of thousands attend the programs on the North and South India tours.

How did this daughter of a fisherman from rural India, who attended school only up to the 4th grade, come to have millions of devotees around the world? How is it that this diminutive Indian lady has hugged over 30 million people, given keynote speeches at the United Nations, received a multitude of awards for her humanitarian activities from governments and distinguished organizations all over the world, been interviewed by many major newspapers and television stations in the United States, and has an award-winning documentary about her life shown at major movie theaters in North America and Europe?

Before Amma's first world tour in 1987, she was virtually unknown outside the state of Kerala, in southwest India. Since then, Amma's popularity has grown as more people recognize her true greatness, many regarding her as the Divine Mother of the Universe, manifesting unconditional divine love. As Jane Goodall, world-renowned primatologist, stated when presenting Amma with the Mahatma Gandhi-Martin Luther King Award for Non-violence at the United Nations in Geneva, "She is God's love in a human body."

Amma's mission has blossomed into an international organization engaged in many spiritual and charitable activities that are helping millions of people. Mother's compassion for the poor led her to assume responsibility for a financially troubled orphanage in Paripally, Kerala, many years ago. More than 400 children were in need of nourishing food and living in filthy buildings on the verge of collapse.

Ashram residents cleaned and improved the facility. Electricity and plumbing were installed, and the children were fed nutritious food. With the material basics taken care of, a comprehensive educational and spiritual program was instituted. Now, the 600 residents regularly win statewide awards for academic and artistic achievements.

Other educational initiatives include the award-winning Amrita University, which includes schools of allopathic and Ayurvedic medicine, dentistry, nursing, pharmacy, engineering, computer technology, business, journalism, and education, as well as many research labs.

There are also more than 50 Amrita Vidyalayam schools throughout India where children learn spiritual values along with academic subjects. Amma has also created special needs schools for hearing-impaired children and special school projects for tribal children. Recently, she initiated a program to provide free education to 30,000 poor children in India.

Other humanitarian initiatives Amma has launched include hospices for the terminally ill, free medical camps, pension programs for 100,000 destitute women, free legal aid, free homes for the homeless poor, and a food distribution program to feed the underprivileged. Under Amma's guidance, more than 70,000 houses for the poor have been built throughout India, including three entire villages rebuilt after the Gujarat earthquake and several thousand houses reconstructed after the tsunami. The Mata Amritanandamayi Math (M.A. Math), her ashram in India, feeds more than two million poor people in India annually through its numerous branches. Throughout the United States, 72,000 meals are provided yearly for the homeless through a program called Mother's Kitchen.

It was Amma's long-held wish that a multi-specialty charity be created. The AIMS (Amrita Institute of Medical Sciences) Hospital in Cochin, Kerala, which opened in 1997, gives high-quality comprehensive medical services to all in need. The former Prime Minister of India, Atal Behari Vajpayee, attended the inauguration of the hospital, which has treated more than 100,000 patients for free and has given millions of dollars' worth of free medical care. In addition to AIMS Hospital, Amma has started many smaller hospitals and hospices throughout India, all of which provide free medical care to the poor.

After the devastating tsunami hit India and Sri Lanka in December 2004, the comprehensive Amrita Tsunami Relief and Rehabilitation Project was launched. In addition to constructing new homes, temporary shelters, and relief camps, the Math also provided scholarships for children, employment for adults, boats for fishermen, free medical care, free psychological counseling, free clothing, and financial support. The M.A. Math also built a bridge connecting the peninsula—where Amritapuri, the headquarters of Amma's international mission, is located—to the mainland, to ensure that the villagers would be able to cross quickly to safety, in the event of another tsunami.

After the disastrous Hurricane Katrina hit the United States in August 2005, the M.A. Math pledged $1 million to the Katrina Relief Fund. Former President Bill Clinton received the check from the M.A. Center. In March 2007, Amma pledged $45 million to curb the high suicide rate among poor farmers in India, precipitated by crop failures and the unbearable burden of debt.

*

In addition to her charitable projects, Amma conducts daily spiritual programs, where she gives her signature embrace to all who come to her, sometimes sitting for 18 hours at a stretch. She is truly an embodiment of unconditional love, devoted to the service of all humanity. People from all walks of life seek Mother out. She receives everyone in the same loving way, regardless of caste or creed. She welcomes all alike, from the wealthy executive to the leprous beggar, from the newborn infant to the wrinkled old man, from the hostile detractor to the ardent admirer. As an untiring servant of all people, her life is dedicated solely to removing the suffering of humanity. No concern is insignificant to her.

Ammachi's (Ammachi means "respected Mother") motherly affection is a soothing balm to all who come to her. Taking each person in her arms without reservation, she is like a mother, bringing solace and peace of mind to all. Her touch is so deeply moving that many burst into tears as they experience the radiance of her divine love and compassion. She teaches by the example of her own life and conveys the highest spiritual truths in the simplest language. She has infused devotion to God, love for fellow beings, and the spirit of selfless service into the hearts of millions.

Sudhamani (Amma's birth name) was born on September 27, 1953, to a poor but pious family in the state of Kerala, on the southwest coast of India. She is the fourth of eight surviving children. At her birth, her family was perplexed by the infant Sudhamani's dark blue complexion. Doctors ruled out disease, and the blue hue on Sudhamani's skin gradually disappeared over the course of her first year. However, her family's aversion to her dark skin marked the beginning of years of ridicule and abuse. Although she underwent much hardship and encountered many obstacles as a child, she continuously sought solace in God.

Adding to the family's bewilderment was Sudhamani's early mastery of Malayalam, her mother tongue. She began speaking when she was six months old, and by age two, Sudhamani was singing songs in praise of Krishna without having received any formal instruction. At the age of five, she began composing songs of deep devotional significance. Her enchanting, soulful singing became well-known throughout the village. Amma has said, "From childhood I had an intense love of the Divine Name. I would repeat the Lord's Name incessantly with every breath, and a constant flow of divine thoughts was kept up in my mind no matter where I was or what I was doing."

As the years passed, Sudhamani spent all her free time immersed in meditation, longing for Krishna. When she was not busy with family chores, people frequently found her sitting with eyes closed, softly singing to God, with tears streaming down her cheeks. Although her family and many of the neighbors were religious, they did not understand Sudhamani's intense spiritual moods, and feared she was insane.

However, childhood friends readily gravitated toward Sudhamani's playful, joyous, and charismatic nature. After finishing her chores, she would tell friends spiritual stories about the playful child Krishna. At these times, her playmates would sing devotional songs composed by Sudhamani.

Required to work long hours in the service of her family when her mother became ill, she could not continue attending school beyond the fourth grade. In addition to looking after all the family household chores, she served the elderly, poor, and sick in her seaside village as if they were members of her own family. She would often surreptitiously take food and clothing from her house and distribute them to those who were poor. One day, not finding anything else, she gave away her mother's only gold bangle to a poor, starving man. She received a severe beating when her father found out, yet she was happy that she could relieve someone's suffering.

Sudhamani's father became more and more concerned about her, fearing that she was insane and worried that her unusual behavior was bringing a bad name to the family. Finally, he locked her out of the family house. When sympathetic local women tried to bring her food and take care of her, they were forbidden to do so by the family. Some of the local villagers who could not understand her state of divine bliss ridiculed her by throwing stones at her and placing thorns where she walked. In spite of all this abuse, Sudhamani remained unperturbed, oblivious to the harassment and physical conditions. She slept outdoors—the sand was her bed, the stars her blanket, and the moon her light. Animals came to feed her—a dog was seen bringing food packets to her, and a cow stood by her side so that she could drink directly from its udder.

One day in September 1975, Sudhamani overheard members of a neighboring family singing devotional songs to Krishna. She was immediately overtaken by divine bliss, and her appearance spontaneously transformed into the features and movements of Lord Krishna. Her skin even took on the blue hue of Lord Krishna. This event marked her first manifestation of *Krishna Bhava,* the Divine Mood of Krishna.

Many people assumed that Krishna had temporarily taken possession of Sudhamani in order to bless them, and news of this rapidly spread throughout the local villages. Skeptics abounded, and one of them demanded that Sudhamani perform a miracle as proof that she was indeed Krishna. She replied, "It is not my intention to show miracles. My goal is to inspire people with the desire for liberation through *realization,* the state of complete identity with God. Miracles are illusory. That is not the essential principle behind spirituality. Not only that, once a miracle is shown, you will desire and demand to see it again and again. I am not here to create desire but to remove it."

Yet, out of compassion toward the villagers and to inspire them with faith, she told them to return in a week, and that she would show them a miracle. The word spread like wildfire among the villagers, and the next week over a thousand people gathered for the event. Sudhamani asked one of the skeptics to bring a pot of water. After a portion was distributed to the devotees, Sudhamani told the skeptic to dip his finger in what remained.

To everyone's amazement, the water turned to milk. The milk was then distributed among the crowd. Sudhamani then called another skeptic and instructed him to dip his finger into the remaining milk. It was immediately transformed into pancham-ritam, a pudding made from milk, honey, bananas, sugar candy, and raisins. This, too, was distributed to the hundreds of people assembled. This event created a vast change in the minds of the people. From that day on, large crowds gathered around her.

On another occasion, a devotee of Ammachi brought her an oil lamp for the little temple in which she received devotees, but her elder brother, one of her greatest antagonists, smashed it. Amma then asked the devotees to bring shells into which water was poured, and a wick was placed in each. She asked the people there to light them, and the flame from these shells lasted the entire night!

However, as the crowds receiving Sudhamani's blessings grew larger, an opposition movement sprang to life, invigorated by those who felt threatened by her not following the traditional role of a woman in India: marrying, bearing children, and staying at home. They ridiculed her, harassed her devotees at every opportunity, and plotted her death.

During *Krishna Bhava*, when Sudhamani would manifest as Krishna, the devotees would offer her milk to drink, since Krishna was fond of milk. One day, an atheist milk vendor secretly added poison to the milk that a devotee bought to offer Sudhamani. Although she knew the milk was poisoned, she did not want to upset the devotee by refusing the offering. So she drank it. Sudhamani immediately became severely ill with stomach pain, but continued the program until every devotee received her blessing, while periodically excusing herself to release the poison from her body.

One day, while Sudhamani was sitting alone in a meditative mood, a beautiful orb of brilliant light appeared before her. As she looked on in wonder, the Divine Mother emerged in an exquisitely beautiful form and then suddenly disappeared along with the light. This vision created in Sudhamani an intense desire to see the Divine Mother again.

After many days of repeating the names of the Goddess Devi ceaselessly and crying out to the Goddess, the Divine Mother at last reappeared before her "in a living form, dazzling like a million suns" and merged in her. Amma stated, "From that point onwards, Amma could see nothing different from her own formless Self in which the entire universe floats like a tiny bubble." Following this experience, Sudhamani withdrew herself from everything and everyone, and remained for days on end immersed in the intense inner bliss of God-consciousness.

One day, she heard a voice from within her say, "I am in all as the One Essence and do not have a particular abode. It is to give solace to the suffering humanity that you have come into this world, and not merely for enjoying Divine Bliss. Therefore, worship Me by showing humanity the way back to Me." This was a turning point in Sudhamani's life. The following days found her fully identified with the loving Divine Mother, and it was from this time onward that people began calling Sudhamani "Amma" or "Mother."

Amma began manifesting *Devi Bhava*, the mood of the Divine Mother, approximately six months after the advent of Krishna Bhava. She would begin the Krishna Bhava program in the early evening, hugging the devotees until midnight, and then, after a short break, the Devi Bhava program would begin and continue until the early morning hours, when the last devotee had received Devi's embrace.

Most villagers assumed that she was temporarily possessed by these deities. But Amma has a different explanation. "All the deities represent the infinite aspects of the One Supreme Being, which exist within us as well. A divine personality can manifest any one of them by his or her mere will for the good of the world. Devi Bhava is the manifestation of the Eternal Feminine; the active principle of the Impersonal Absolute.

"It should be remembered that all objects having a name or form are mere mental projections. Why should a doctor wear a white coat, or a policeman a uniform and cap? All these are merely external aids meant to create a certain impression. In a like manner, Amma dons the garb of Devi in order to give strength to the devotional attitude of the people. The Universal Spirit that is in me is also within you. If you can realize that Indivisible Principle that is ever shining in you, you will become one with That."

Although there have been numerous miraculous healings associated with Amma, the real miracle is her unconditional love, which she manifests constantly. Amma is not interested in changing anyone's religion, but simply wishes to lead people to Love, the heart of all faiths.

Since 1981, the Holy Mother has been disseminating spiritual knowledge to thousands of spiritual aspirants who have come to live in her ashram, training them with practical spiritual discipline. She has stated that the greatest of all blessings is to realize the glory of the divinity within. There are currently several thousand permanent residents living in the Amritapuri ashram.

*

I have been blessed to be able to live in the M.A. Center in California since 1995 (the M.A. Center is Amma's main ashram in the United States). Located in the San Francisco Bay Area, the

M.A. Center is where Amma spends more time than anywhere except Amritapuri. Amma's divine energy permeates the land where she has walked.

It is said that the ashram is the body of the Guru. So anything positive in this book that touches your heart comes from the fact that I have been living at the M.A. Center while writing this book.

Amma's incredible ability to serve the poor and suffering humanity virtually 24 hours a day every day of the year is further evidence of her being a *mahatma* (great soul). As a matter of fact, there has never been a saint who has demonstrated God's unconditional love by hugging thousands of people daily. May Amma's constant selfless acts continue to uplift suffering humanity and serve as a beacon of light and inspiration to her millions of devotees.

Amma blessing her little children

Chapter 1

The Omniscient Guru

"The omniscient Guru will gradually take the disciple to the goal. Attachment to the Guru's form, supported by the awareness of his omniscience and all-pervasiveness, is the perfect attitude. The Guru's sole intention is to improve the disciple. The Guru will observe each and every action of the disciple but the disciple will not know it."

— Amma

The 93rd mantra from the 108 names of the Holy Mother: "Salutations to Amma, who sees all the actions of the disciple."

Amma Can Speak and Understand All Languages

A friend of mine, a Hindi-speaking Indian woman, her husband, and two sisters-in-law met Mother for the first time several years ago at the San Ramon ashram. Hindi and Malayalam, Amma's native tongue, are as different as English and German. Each family member had a question they wanted to ask Amma, but I told them that she doesn't answer questions during the evening darshan.

I further mentioned that Amma is omniscient and knows what is in our hearts and minds, and recommended that the family internally ask Amma for help when they received their darshan. The first woman inwardly prayed to Amma for help with some challenges she was having in her marriage. Amma exclaimed in Hindi, "Don't worry darling daughter, I'll take care of your marriage."

When her husband was in front of Amma, he silently noted how worried he was about his mother and wished his turbulent mind would settle down. Amma told the man in Hindi, "Don't worry about your mother; your mind will become peaceful."

One sister-in-law prayed internally to Amma that her son's leg would get better. Amma again responded in the woman's native tongue, "Your son will be okay."

The other sister-in-law was concerned that she still wasn't married. Amma stated in Hindi, "You will get married." The delighted and awestruck family blissfully left their darshan amazed that Amma not only knew their every thought, but gave them advice and encouragement in their native tongue.

*

A woman from Yugoslavia came to India to see Amma many years ago. She was devastated emotionally since she had lost her husband and parents during her country's recent civil war. She told one of the swamis that because of the language barrier, she was afraid that Amma wouldn't understand her.

When the woman went up for her first darshan, Amma began gently singing to her, and suddenly the new devotee burst into tears. Later, the woman told the swami that Amma sang an old Yugoslavian folk song that she had not heard since her childhood, when her own mother would sing it to her. The words of the song were, "Be happy, the world is as insubstantial as a dream. Don't let life make you sad."

The elated woman returned to her homeland a few weeks later with peace in her heart and a new outlook on life.

Amma Fulfills Innocent Desires

Durga, a humble young woman from Brazil, was born with a congenital eye disease. She came to see Amma for her first darshan several years ago. Her specific ailment generally creates blindness by early adulthood. In fact, a cousin of hers who has the same disease and is in his 20s is already blind. When Durga was in the darshan line waiting for her hug from Amma, she was sobbing, praying for Amma to help her. As Durga approached Amma, Mother told her in Portuguese, "Don't cry, don't cry," and put a yellow cloth on her head as if she were initiating Durga. Amma then spontaneously began rubbing Durga's eyes and later told her not to worry about her eyes. Not only did she not become blind, through Amma's grace she became the first foreign student to graduate from AIMS Medical College.

Once, when Durga went for darshan after she began attending medical school, Amma told her, "Send the picture of yourself to your parents." Durga could not understand what Amma was referring to and asked, "What picture?" The following week, there was a story in a local Malayalam newspaper and along with it was a picture of Durga sitting next to Amma. Durga happily sent the photo to her proud parents.

One day, outside the AIMS hospital in Cochin, Durga innocently picked a bud from a bush before the flower had a chance to bloom, because she couldn't find a flower for her altar where she worshipped Amma. A supervisor at the hospital saw her picking the bud and severely scolded her, telling her that she had committed a sin by picking the bud before it had a chance to bloom. Durga felt bad about this. Since she had already picked the bud, she felt that she should go ahead and put it at Amma's feet on her altar. The next day, instead of wilting, she saw that the bud had blossomed into a magnificent, huge flower that emitted a beautiful fragrance.

One day in Amritapuri, Durga had an intense desire to see Amma. However, there was no darshan scheduled that day, so she decided to sit on the stairs that led to Amma's room. While sitting there, a thought arose in her mind, that it would be special to be able to swim with Amma. She fasted that entire day, waiting hopefully for just a glance of the Divine Mother. By the afternoon, Durga was beginning to feel despondent that her desire would not be fulfilled, when a *brahmacharini* (female renunciant) came from Amma's room looking for Durga. She said that Amma was calling her. When Durga reached Amma's room, Mother invited Durga to go swimming with her, thereby fulfilling her innocent desire.

During Durga's first year in medical school, she was having many challenges adjusting to the new environment and her arduous studies. One day, she decided to go to the cafeteria to relax and eat a nice lunch. While eating her meal, she noticed a scrumptious-looking banana lying on the table. She had an overwhelming desire to eat the fruit but did not do so, thinking that it probably belonged to another student. However, throughout the day she had thoughts of how satisfying it would be to eat a banana. Later that day, when she returned to her locked room, she was mystified to find a banana lying on her altar next to a picture of Amma's feet.

*

When Mother was in Calicut, India, in December 2002, she blessed tens of thousands of devotees daily, which meant that each person could receive only a three-second darshan, just enough time for Amma to give a quick embrace, whisper "my

28

darling son" or "my darling daughter" into their ear, and give them *prasad* (sacred offering, usually food blessed by the Guru). During the quick darshan, one man blurted out that he had traveled 200 kilometers to see her. Mother then motioned for him to sit down near her. He prayed to be able to ask Amma a question, but with Amma's continuous three-second darshans, he felt that it wouldn't be possible. After about 10 minutes, Amma turned toward him and quickly uttered, "You want to ask me about your sister's wedding. Don't worry. Mother will take care of everything."

*

In spite of these marathon darshan sessions with tens of thousands of devotees, Amma remembers everyone who comes for darshan. Several years ago, there was another huge crowd in Calicut; Amma blessed tens of thousands of people during a three-day program. A few days later, Amma asked about an ashram driver, inquiring as to why he hadn't come for darshan when he was in Calicut.

*

Every Tuesday in Amritapuri, ashram residents and guests receive prasad lunch from the hands of Amma herself. An elderly, diabetic Indian woman resident of the ashram was supposed to be on a diet. Before attending that morning's meditation and satsang with Amma, she had brought three *idlis* (steamed rice cakes) to her room from the ashram breakfast. When Amma gave her a small portion for lunch, she asked for more food. Amma responded that she could eat the three idlis she had kept in her room.

*

A devotee who lived near Amritapuri would lovingly offer hot milk to the picture of Amma on his altar everyday. Part of his daily ritual included cooling down the milk so that when he offered the libation to Amma, it would be as if she were directly sipping the hot beverage. However, one day the devotee was in a hurry and didn't have time to cool down the milk. Later that day, when he arrived at the ashram for darshan, he noticed a burn blister on Amma's lips. Mother told him, "Next time you offer Amma milk, cool it down."

*

A friend of mine, Lakshmi, came to the M.A. Center in San Ramon, California, to receive a mantra from Amma during Devi Bhava several years ago. I had had a blissful experience with Amma earlier that evening and was ready to go to sleep. The hall was very crowded with devotees standing and sitting everywhere.

As I walked toward the back of the hall to leave, I saw Lakshmi, who had just received a mantra. She looked like she was in another world and barely murmured the word "dizzy." Suddenly she fainted, and I reached out to catch her. I then supported her on a chair for about five minutes.

Finally, with the help of the security staff and a nurse, we managed to take her to a nearby cottage. As she lay on a mat, she would slowly open her eyes at times, but then drift back into another world. When we were trying to revive her, a Malayalam-speaking Indian woman doctor came into the room to check on her condition. It turned out that even though no one told Amma what had transpired, Amma was aware of Lakshmi's need for medical help and summoned the doctor. Amma told the doctor, "One of my daughters needs some help and she is in the cottage!" Finally, after some time, Lakshmi returned to full consciousness and had a friend drive her home.

*

When my friend Robert went for darshan several years ago, his wife did not go along with him because of work obligations. She asked him to think of her when he received his blessing. Mother whispered into his ear "my darling son" three times, followed by "my darling daughter" three times.

*

After meeting Amma, Bala, a devotee, followed Amma to many cities on the U.S. tour. During one program, he was sitting at the back of the hall and feeling sad, thinking that even though he had been following Amma from city to city, she didn't even know his name. As he was lost in this reverie, suddenly another devotee, Prema, whom he had just met the day before, tapped him on his shoulder. She told him that as she was getting up after receiving darshan, Amma told her to ask Bala to come sit near Mother.

*

A devotee from New Zealand was visiting the San Ramon ashram for the first time during Amma's June tour a few years ago. Mike was quite a *sevak* (someone who does selfless service) and had been working hard all day, digging holes for some posts. He hadn't eaten all day and by 4 p.m. he was exhausted. While doing his seva, he had the thought that he wished Amma knew how hard he had been working all day. When he finally went for darshan that night after dinner, Amma asked him, "Stomach full and muscles tired?"

Amma Knows her Children's Thoughts, Whether They Are Near or Far

In June 1997, while sitting near Amma one morning and watching her hug devotees, she called me for darshan with the wave of her hand, something that she had never done before. The previous night, I had visited Shakti, a longtime devotee and ashram resident who was in the hospital recovering from cancer and was having a difficult time with chemotherapy. He had said that he was feeling very sad that instead of being with Amma at the San Ramon ashram, he was suffering in the hospital, and was feeling disconnected from Amma. The two of us were alone in his hospital room when his stomach began to feel sick. However, later during the visit, he began to feel much better physically.

When I went for darshan, Mother asked me, "Yesterday Shakti felt sick in the stomach in the hospital, but then felt better?"

This was Amma's way of letting Shakti and me know that she had been with him in the hospital, and was blessing and healing him.

*

Several years ago my niece, Puneeta, and I were briefly visiting Amma's host family's house in Chicago when Mother arrived. While Amma was compassionately stroking the arm of a Malayalam-speaking boy with Down's Syndrome and talking to him sweetly for some time, my niece was thinking that she was sad that she couldn't understand Malayalam, Amma's native tongue. Amma asked the boy to sing a bhajan and she burst out laughing in joy when the boy repeatedly yelled "Amma, Amma." When Mother got up to leave the room, she walked up to Puneeta and grabbed her hand and told her in English, "Don't be sad when Mother speaks Malayalam."

The following week, Puneeta was feeling heartbroken that she couldn't see Amma in New York in July and wouldn't be seeing her again till she returned to the U.S. the following November. I talked to Puneeta on the phone right before I went up for darshan during Devi Bhava in New York. Puneeta ended our conversation by saying, "Send her all my love."

However, when I went up for darshan, I forgot what Puneeta asked me to tell Mother and instead told her that I was returning to the San Ramon ashram the following day. Amma's response was "Sister's daughter, send her my love." I always get nervous when Amma speaks to me, and I didn't understand what she was trying to say. I just stared at her like a dummy.

She then looked me right in the eye and clearly stated, "You are not understanding me." Finally Gita, Amma's attendant who stands next to Mother, told me, "Amma is referring to your relative from Chicago." Then Amma and I both said Chicago at the same moment as she repeated, "Send her all my love."

Because I had told Amma that I was returning to San Ramon, I wasn't surprised that she gave me prasad of some chocolate kisses to give to the ashram residents who were not able to go on the tour. During the previous conversation while Mother was looking straight at me, she reached over and grabbed some candies from the prasad tray and placed them in my hand. After that glorious darshan, I sat down and meditated for some time. When I opened my eyes I decided to count the pieces of chocolate kisses. I counted eight pieces of candy, which I later realized was the exact number of ashram residents who had stayed in San Ramon.

The following year Amma performed a marriage ceremony for Puneeta to a wonderful and compassionate Indian man named

Jai. I had a secret desire that the two families would get blessed together during Amma's visit in Chicago before the wedding; a coming together of East and West under the holy auspices of the Divine Mother. However, every time we all tried to have darshan together it was either too crowded or one of the family members was not available. At the end of the wedding, Amma specifically brought Jai, Puneeta, Sharda (Jai's mom), and me together for a group blessing, thereby fulfilling my desire.

*

Devi, a longtime American devotee of Amma, had briefly lived in Amritapuri, where she met her German husband. However, after some time, the marriage had ended. Devi had continued to live in Germany, but she wasn't sure if she should stay in Germany or return to the United States. One June morning, as Devi pondered her future, she was walking down a busy city street when all of a sudden she entered a dreamlike state: her movements went into slow motion and her thoughts disappeared. At that moment, she heard a clear voice state, "Go back to America." She just dismissed the voice, thinking it was her ego telling her to return to the United States since she wasn't sure if that was really the right move. Amma was on the U.S. tour at that time. Devi emailed her friend who was planning to see Amma in California, to ask Mother where Devi should live. Amma's surprising response was, "I already told her to go back to America."

*

Amma also made Her divine presence known to me when I was in Europe recently on business. Many years before I had joined an international peace group, Servas, whereby travelers meet local people in an attempt to establish common connections, to promote world peace. During this trip, I only had time to meet one Servas Danish family that resided in a small town north of Copenhagen.

When the Danish Servas host, Hans, met me at the train station, we went to a local market to buy food for dinner. He was disappointed when I told him that I didn't eat meat, but then he asked, "You drink beer don't you?" I responded no and when I also said that I didn't drink wine either, he looked at me like I was very strange. I then inwardly asked Amma, "What am I doing here?" I began feeling very uncomfortable and didn't really want to go to his house.

When we arrived at the house, his wife, Kara, told Hans that his daughter (by a previous marriage) was in a crisis because her boyfriend had left her and she had expressed some suicidal thoughts. I uncomfortably sat down on the couch in the living room as Hans nervously called his daughter, and I awkwardly tried to make conversation with Kara. After some time, Kara mentioned that she took a weekly yoga class. I enthusiastically responded that I also study yoga and Kara asked where I take the classes. I told her that I take classes at a meditation center, which is called an ashram, where I also live. When Kara inquired what the name of the ashram was, I told her that she probably wouldn't have heard of my spiritual teacher, Amma.

Surprisingly, she said that she had old friends who had met Amma and who had emigrated from Denmark to Canada. She then asked me if I knew her friends. I told her that tens of thousands of people visit Amma every year in North America and I was sure I wouldn't know her friends. As she described her friends, I spontaneously asked Kara if her friends had a son. Suddenly, I realized that not only did I know her friends, but that their son had been in my preteen group many years ago during the programs at the San Ramon ashram. Kara then showed me a copy of the biography of Amma that her friend had sent her. We all had a wonderful evening together and I felt so blessed that Amma had guided me to these hosts. My sharing some of Amma's teachings seemed to have helped Hans deal with the familial crises.

What are the odds that strangers in a little Danish village would have Amma's biography in their house? Only a hundred percent with a great mahatma like Amma as the Guru.

Ashram Delivery from a UPS (Understanding Principles of Spirituality) Driver

Since the M.A. Center is the main clearing-house for Amma's products in North America, we frequently receive truck deliveries at the ashram. One UPS driver, a very nice Peruvian man, had made one delivery to the ashram before Amma's recent November tour to San Ramon. During that first delivery I had shared with him some information about Amma and how she was helping the poor in India. He told me that he was also involved in an organization trying to help the poor in his native Peru.

On his second delivery to the ashram several months later, I happened to be walking by the temple where he was dropping off pallets of boxes for the bookstore. I told the driver a little bit more about Amma and gave him a brochure about Amma's charitable activities. When he saw the picture of Amma on the brochure he suddenly became very serious as he stared at the photo of Mother.

In a shaky voice he told me, "That lady (pointing to Amma's picture) came to me last night in a dream! When I woke up, I still saw her in my mind's eye, wearing a white sari."

Amma's beautiful ashram in San Ramon, California

He didn't know what to make of the experience, but when he had reported to work that morning, he was "coincidentally" told to make a delivery to the M.A. Center, which he remembered was an Indian ashram. He became quite excited as he read the literature I gave him about Amma and said he looked forward to meeting her in June. I've met several people over the years who have also told me that Amma had come to them in a dream before they met her in person.

Amma, the Divine Publisher

Since I have a sensitive nervous system, I became interested in a book entitled *The Highly Sensitive Person.* Highly sensitive people comprise 20 percent of the population and have trouble screening out stimuli such as noise, bright lights, and strong smells. Highly sensitive people are also easily overwhelmed by crowds, and time pressure. I've been dealing with my finely tuned nervous system my entire life.

With the encouragement of my niece, Puneeta, I decided to write a book entitled *The Highly Sensitive Person's Survival Guide*, about essential skills for living well in an overstimulating world. After receiving six rejections from literary agents, in September 2003 I received a call from an acquisitions editor at New Harbinger Publications stating that he was interested in publishing the book. However, after a company meeting a few days later, he told me that his sales staff wasn't sure if the book would be marketable. I then tried to contact the editor for more than a month, leaving many messages. Since I received no response from the editor, I gave up hope that New Harbinger would publish the book.

When Amma was in San Ramon that November, I told her what had transpired and asked if I should still try to contact other publishers or print the book myself. She responded, "If the first company doesn't publish the book, you could try other companies, or print the book yourself."

However, an hour after talking to Amma about publishing the book, I received a call from the acquisitions editor at New Harbinger. To my utter surprise, he informed me that New Harbinger would publish the book. This experience was another lesson to help me realize that everything happens by Amma's grace.

Amma, the Divine Employment Counselor

Several years ago, my friend Bala was informed that he was soon going to be laid off from his job in the Bay Area. Since engineering jobs were difficult to find at the time, he felt that only Amma's intervention could help him. Because Amma was on her European tour then, he used the Internet to find the city Amma was visiting and called the phone number listed under contact information. He knew that the chances were very slim that the busy host would even answer the phone as Amma was already giving programs there. However, when he called, the host answered the phone and Bala asked if he could speak to Swami Ramakrishnananda (one of Amma's monastic disciples) who "happened" to be standing next to the phone. Swamiji told Bala that he would inform Mother about Bala losing his job.

When Bala called back half an hour later Swami Ramakrishnananda told Bala that as soon as he entered Amma's room, before Swamiji could tell her what happened, Amma said, "Bala just called and is worried about his job situation." She further stated, "He shouldn't worry. Amma will take care of everything."

A week later when Bala was finally told that he was laid off from his job, he was smiling because he had total faith that Mother would help him find a new job. He came to the San Ramon ashram a few weeks later to do seva and the wife of an engineer asked him if he knew of anyone who was looking for work who happened to have the exact skills that Bala possessed. He got the new job on the 29th day after he was laid off; if it had been 30 days he would have had visa problems.

*

Amma is always very practical when she gives career advice. She also cautions us to use discrimination before pursuing a specific occupation. When Amma was visiting San Ramon in November some years ago, I had been offered two different jobs during the previous week. When I asked her which job I should take, she responded, "Take the job that pays the most, but allows you to spend time with Amma." Her answer effectively eliminated one of the jobs since it offered only two weeks of vacation a year, which would not have allowed me to travel with Amma.

Amma, the One Who Manifests in Flowers and Fruit

Buvenesh, a devotee who lives near the San Ramon ashram, was sitting on his mother's front porch on a beautiful spring day a few years ago watching some lovely snow-white petals that had dropped from the blossoms of a nearby apple tree. He suddenly became filled with divine joy and felt Amma's presence well up in his heart. Buvenesh had recently learned the IAM meditation technique (Integrated Amrita Meditation, a meditation technique Amma created) and began reflecting on how the IAM meditation had helped him to grow spiritually.

Lost in a reverie of appreciation, he happened to gaze down at one of the soft petals that had landed in front of him on the porch. He was astonished when he noticed that engraved on the flower in a perfect delicate print were three letters: I A M. Later in the week, Buvenesh showed me the petal that he had carefully placed in a plastic bag. It was truly an awesome sight to see the letters I A M engraved in the delicate tiny white petal.

*

A few ashram residents were present when Br. (abbreviation for "brahmachari") Dayamrita led a *puja* (ritual worship) for the new Amrita TV studio that had been recently constructed in the main house of the San Ramon ashram. The puja setup included the customary fruit and flowers placed on the altar in front of Amma's picture.

When the short yet inspiring puja was completed, the devotees left the studio and went to the kitchen for dinner. A few minutes later one of the residents, Jukka, entered the kitchen with a pear. He said that he picked the pear up after the puja and

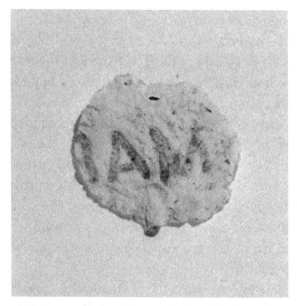

Flower petal that Bhuvanesh found with IAM
written on it while longing to be with Amma.

noticed a perfect OM sign was imprinted on it. As the devotees incredulously passed the fruit around, staring at the OM sign, we were deeply appreciative of this clear sign of Amma's presence during the puja ceremony.

Amma, the Divine Weather Forecaster

During Amma's November visit to the California ashram, parking is especially challenging because more people come in November than in June. Also, there is the possibility of rain, which can turn some of our large hilly parking lots into slippery, muddy fields.

A few years ago, Amma asked Br. Dayamrita why the parking staff was not parking cars on the grassy hills across the street that morning. He said that as it was supposed to rain, the slope would become too slippery. Amma then asked him how he knew that it was going to rain, and he responded that the weather forecast on TV, radio and the Internet all predicted rain. She replied that he could choose to believe the TV, radio and the Internet if he wanted to, implying that he was talking to a higher source of weather prediction at that moment.

Br. Dayamrita relayed Amma's weather forecast to the parking staff. Based on the conversation with Amma, the parking staff parked cars on the hilly lots for the Devi Bhava program that afternoon. Even though the weather forecast had stated that there was 90 percent chance of heavy rains during Devi Bhava, there was no rain at all-so we could use all the parking lots we had, allowing as many devotees as possible to receive the blessings of the Divine Mother.

Amma, being one with God, cannot only accurately predict the weather, but can create the weather. One year when Amma went to Santa Fe, New Mexico the city was in the midst of one of their longest droughts, and when Mother arrived, it "mysteriously" began to rain.

Amma, the Divine Astrologer

Amma, being omnipresent, is aware of the contents of everyone's astrology chart. Several years ago, I asked Amma if I should go into business with another devotee who lived in a different state. Amma responded, "He is going through a difficult astrological period. So, be careful with this business." I then began working with another devotee in the same business, rationalizing that Amma didn't say the other devotee was in a bad astrological period. However, I was actually ignoring Amma's warning to be careful with this business, and since the two devotees were working with each other, the venture turned out to be a financial disaster.

I have been doing Vedic astrology readings at the M.A. Center since 1998. I think that the only reason some of my clients may have had a beneficial reading is due to the fact that I do the readings at Amma's ashram. The ashram is the body of the Guru and before each reading, I pray to Amma for guidance to help each soul.

*

Most astrologers ask their clients to repeat planetary mantras to lessen the malefic effects of inauspicious planets. Several years ago, I asked Amma if it was okay to tell my clients which mantras to repeat. She responded, "You can recommend pujas but not mantras since you will take on the karma of the person by giving them mantras." I offer my *pranams* (salutations) again and again to Amma, our omniscient Guru, who is always protecting her devotees.

Amma has said that for a disciple who is truly surrendered to the Guru, one's astrology chart ceases to matter. In the next breath she added, "Who is truly surrendered to the Guru?" However, I have noticed that even during very difficult astrological periods, when I have been in Amma's physical presence the challenges abate.

When Saturn is in transit over the Moon, something that happens every 29 years, it can be a very difficult time for that person. I have noticed that frequently people contact me for readings at that time in their lives. Prior to one tour, Saturn transited my Moon for six solid weeks. Although there were no particular new, outward difficulties in my life during that period, as soon as Saturn moved to within a degree of my Moon, I became severely anxious and sad. However, during the week Amma was in San

Ramon I felt great. When I was no longer in her physical presence, I again began feeling anxious and sad.

*

Before Amma's arrival in San Ramon one year, I had been going through a very challenging Saturn time period that had begun in September. I believed that employing astrological remedial measures would help offset the negative results of the yearlong Saturn time period. Therefore, I began going to a nearby Hindu temple to do puja and *archana* (recitation of the names of the Divine Mother), and repeat planetary mantras. I had just completed an elaborate Navagraha puja to all nine planets, which was expensive and quite complex. I also planned on going to the Hindu temple every Saturday (since Saturn rules Saturdays) to perform archana, puja, and mantras to Saturn.

However, Amma told me that going to the Hindu temple to propitiate the planets was not necessary. She instructed me that all I needed to do was repeat the mantra she had given me, do archana, and help the poor. At that moment, I deeply realized that Amma's will is the cosmic will, and that by following her instructions I am propitiating the cosmic will.

Amma created the Brahmasthanam temples, which are special temples that beautifully illustrate the essential principles of unity in diversity. They are the first Indian temples to show multiple deities carved on a single stone. Amma created the Brahmasthanam temples in India to remove obstacles in her devotees' lives and to alleviate suffering. So, for my clients, I highly recommend having pujas performed at Amma's Brahmasthanam temples when they are going through a difficult astrological time period. For those devotees outside India, pujas can be arranged by visiting the Puja page on the amma.org website.

Amma Is Always Calling Her Children

A few weeks after my last darshan with Amma during the 2011 summer tour, I was house-sitting for a friend who had just had an operation to remove tumors in her body. After eating a light breakfast, I became lost in a daydream, reflecting that I had only seen Amma a few weeks earlier, but that now, as I tried to stay warm on a cold, foggy Berkeley morning, it seemed like ages since I had been in her divine presence. I felt so disconnected from Amma and deeply sad that she was so far away from me. Interrupting my dismal reverie, my friend's phone rang, forcing me to return to the present moment from my far away thoughts.

Suddenly I heard a familiar voice on the answering machine: "This is Swami Amritswarupananda (affectionately known as Swamiji). Amma wants to talk to you right now."

Was this Amma calling in response to my lonely daydream? Or perhaps this was just a continuation of my reverie where Amma comes to me. I doubted that it could be real, but as I continued to hear Swamiji's voice, I suddenly bolted up from the chair. This was no dream. It was actually Amma calling from Toronto, to talk to my friend and find out how the surgery had gone. I quickly raced to pick up the phone and shouted, "Namah Shivaya," not knowing which buttons to push to turn off the answering machine so Swamiji could hear me. Then I found myself listening to the sweet sounds of *bhajans* (devotional singing) playing in the background and Amma's voice talking with various people as she gave darshan in Toronto.

Swamiji apparently thought I was my friend's husband, and said, "Amma wants to talk with you now." But before he could give the phone to Amma, I responded, "Swamiji, this is Dayalu." I added that my friend was still in the hospital and I was house-sitting for her. I then proceeded to get Swamiji's phone number so that my friend could call him back so that she could talk to Amma.

When Amma finally spoke to my friend, she gave very up-lifting and practical advice on how to proceed with treating her illness. Amma inspired her with so much encouragement that both she and her husband were transformed.

Amma can change our despair to bliss in a split second. Since Amma is truly always within us, let us listen closely for that divine ring in our heart and always keep our line open to receive the nectar of her divine love.

Chapter II

The Divine Qualities of a Mahatma

"Spiritual power is always radiating from a mahatma. This creates spiritual energy in us when we sit in his presence. A mahatma exemplifies God's divine qualities of love, compassion, and inner peace."

– Amma

Strong as a Boulder, Light as a Feather

Once, when a devotee expressed concern for Amma's health after she gave darshan for 14 hours, she replied that if her body were made of steel, it would have broken a long time ago. On Amma's tours in India, she sometimes consecrates Brahmasthanam temples. At one such consecration ceremony, four men were carrying a very heavy stone statue into the inner temple, where Mother was preparing for the ceremony. As the devotees were carrying the bulky statue through the door, one of them slipped and was about to drop the sculpture. He yelled out, "Amma!" Mother came over quickly and supported the idol with one hand and picked up the devotee with the other.

On another occasion, Amma was traveling in a van to a program with some devotees. One devotee sitting next to Amma was in awe of her good fortune to be able to sit next to the Divine Mother. However, the devotee had severe knee problems and was a little concerned that someone in the van might sit close to her and push against her knees, which would cause her great pain. Suddenly, Amma exclaimed that she wanted to sit on the lap of that devotee, who became frightened that Amma's weight might cause irreparable damage to her knees. Yet, even though Amma sat in her lap, the devotee reported that much to her amazement she felt no pain at all; it was as if Amma had made herself weightless!

Sacrificing Her Well-Being for Her Children's Sake

After the evening bhajans in San Ramon, Amma used to have to walk down a flight of stairs from the stage to the main part of

Amma ascending to the stage for an evening program in San Ramon

the hall, to begin giving darshan. One night during a November program, I was blessed to help Amma down the stairs. I held out my hand and Amma leaned on my hand as she descended the steps. Suddenly, a little five-year-old boy tried to grab Amma's hand. I was concerned that the little boy couldn't support Amma walking down the stairs, so I still held on to her hand. But Amma told me, "Let the boy hold my hand. He wants to help Amma." I let go of Amma's hand immediately but as soon as I let go of Mother's hand she started to wobble, so I quickly grabbed her hand again to support her so she wouldn't fall down the stairs.

Even though Amma stumbled by letting the little boy help her, she again requested that the boy continue to help her to her chair. Fulfilling the boy's innocent desire was clearly more important than actually being supported as she walked.

I have seen people put their knees on Amma's feet as they kneel to receive darshan. Rather than react to the pain she must feel, an expression that might upset the person, Amma smiles at the devotee.

*

During the beginning of her 1999 summer tour, Mother was experiencing some pain in her body, and several devotees expressed a great deal of concern about her ability to continue giving darshan.

When Mother arrived in the white van at the guest house for the retreat at Fort Flagler (an old army base outside of Seattle that had been converted into a beautiful park and retreat center), I was asked to put my hand out so she could be supported in case she needed help getting out of the van. I was shocked to experience her full weight leaning on me as she slowly and painfully stepped down from the vehicle. She appeared to have difficulty walking as she gradually made her way toward the two-story white clapboard house. I was very worried that after more than 20 years of people constantly putting their weight on her small body, she would finally be unable to continue hugging her millions of devotees all over the world.

Before the evening program began, I decided to stand near the stage, to help Mother up the five steps to the stage. I wondered how she could possibly ascend the stairs, given the difficulty she appeared to be experiencing earlier in the day just getting out of the van. However, as Amma entered the darshan hall it appeared that every cell of her body was radiating joy and bliss, in such stark contrast to what she had exhibited a few hours earlier. She smiled at all the devotees as she moved swiftly toward the stage. I put my hand out as she approached the steps, but she waved me away as she bounded up the stairs, full of energy.

Even though Amma appeared physically better during the Seattle retreat, by the time she arrived in San Ramon a few days later, some disciples told me that Amma was in so much pain that she was wearing a neck brace, and that she was going to give a new type of darshan, a change they recommended since they thought it would be too painful for her to hug devotees.

I was informed that Mother would just touch the devotees' third eye, rather than give them her usual embrace. I waited expectantly as the first devotee approached Mother for darshan, wondering what this new type of darshan would look like. However, as the first devotee approached, Amma tore off her neck brace, grabbed the devotee, and hugged her tightly.

Great mahatmas like Amma are not subject to every whim and need of their body. We may foolishly think that we are helping her physically, but it is her will that is always helping us on every level.

Salutations to Amma, Whose Stomach Becomes Full When Others Have Their Meals

(mantra 32, Amma's *Ashtottaram*-recitation
of the 108 names of Amma)

Frequently, devotees urge Amma to eat some food, since she often has no time to eat anything. However, Swami Paramatmananda, Amma's first Western swami, witnessed something a long time ago that made him realize her body is not like an ordinary human body and does not need as much food as ordinary people for sustenance.

Seeing that she hadn't eaten for a long time, Nealu (as the swami was called then) urged Amma to eat something. After his incessant pleading, Amma finally relented, and told him to bring some *appams* (rice pancakes). After eating that, she asked for some more and then more food. After eating four or five plates of food, she asked for yet more. As Swami had to walk to a teashop in the village in order to bring her more food, he was becoming tired. Having finally understood that Amma's body didn't require food in the same way that ordinary people do, he pleaded with her to stop so that he could rest a little. Swami learned that if Amma ate nothing or a lot, her consumption of food wasn't important, as long as her children were fed.

Powerhouse of Energy

A few years ago at the San Ramon ashram, Devi Bhava ended at 11:30 a.m., approximately 16 hours after the program had begun. Amma had arrived at the hall the previous evening at 6:30 p.m. and had begun giving darshan at 8 p.m. without any break, as usual. She looked very tired at the end of darshan, with her golden, tear-stained sari smeared with the sweat and makeup of her devotees.

A few hours later, Amma left her room to visit the home of a devotee before going to the airport to fly back to India. I was amazed to see Amma when she came out of her room just hours after the marathon Devi Bhava ended. She looked radiant, as if she had just been refreshed by a long, good night's sleep. Her eyes were sparkling as she affectionately kissed each ashram resident. Amma is a dynamo of energy since she is always connected to the eternal power source.

Always Centered

During a recent U.S. tour, I witnessed a strange event next to Amma, while she was giving darshan in Iowa. There are signs throughout the darshan hall stating that taking pictures is prohibited. The ashram has its own photographers, who take pictures that are later checked by Amma before they are sold. The sale of the pictures supports Amma's charitable activities.

Suddenly, a woman pushed her way to the front of the darshan line holding a disposable camera. She handed the camera to one of the brahmacharis and asked him to take her picture with Amma. Many devotees became agitated, seeing the woman's audacious behavior. She pushed her face next to Amma who was giving darshan, and impudently told Amma to face the camera and smile.

Seeing this disrespectful behavior, many of us became very upset. However, Amma just smiled and gestured that it was all right. After the woman told Amma she wanted another picture taken, she went to the side of Amma's chair and demanded to know who had her camera. Grabbing her camera, she quickly walked out of the darshan hall. Although the devotees were disturbed, Amma, who is always centered in God-consciousness, never looked dismayed for a moment.

One Who Loves to Laugh

One evening in San Ramon, the devotee giving a talk told a funny story about a Chinese monk who put firecrackers in his clothes before he died so that when he was to be cremated, the firecrackers would explode, making everyone laugh, illustrating that there can be humor even in death. When she heard the story, Amma laughed out loud for quite a while as she clapped her hands in delight.

After the speaker ended his talk, Amma asked the devotees if they wanted a question-and-answer session or *bhajans* (devotional singing). As enthusiastic devotees shouted that they wanted a question-and-answer session, Swami Amritaswarupananda (referred to as Swamiji) said that if Amma gave talks every night, we would not be able to digest her sacred words and would get indigestion. I whispered to Swami Amritatmananda, who was sitting next to me, "We want indigestion." He asked me to shout what I had whispered to him. I was too embarrassed to yell, but he said that Amma just looked at me, indicating that she wanted to hear what I said. So I shouted, "We want indigestion!" Amma burst out laughing and said, "Laughter is the best satsang."

One Who Always Helps Others

Amma is always thinking about how to help her children 24/7, without a thought of her own needs. Even when Amma is not giving darshan to the thousands of devotees who come for a hug, she is meeting coordinators of her multiple charitable activities or answering the hundreds of daily letters sent to her. Amma's mind is always focused on helping both those who are with her physically, and those who are not. I remember when some of the devotees met Amma in Seattle before the start of one summer tour, she said that we should now spend some time thinking of those devotees who were not with Amma and also those devotees who had passed on.

*

When Amma left the San Ramon ashram in June 2007, I noticed a small picture that Amma had drawn in her room, of two people in a boat, in which it appeared that one person was rowing the other across the ocean. Even when Mother is alone she is always focused on bringing her children across the ocean of *samsara* (cycle of birth and death) to the shores of divine bliss.

*

In June 2005, six months after the devastating tsunami struck the coasts of South India and other parts of Asia, Amma had returned to her room after giving darshan to thousands of devotees during the first morning program at the San Ramon ashram. There were only a few hours until the evening program and most of the tour staff were looking forward to resting for a few hours, showering, and eating. However, Amma is never concerned with her own physical needs.

Br. (abbreviation for "brahmachari," a celibate male disciple who practices spiritual disciplines under a Guru's guidance; "Bri." or "brahmacharini" is the female equivalent) Dayamrita wanted to make sure that Amma would rest before the evening program, but when he entered Amma's room, she began talking to him about the condition of the tsunami victims and about all the relief and rehabilitation work that needed to be completed. She continued talking for several hours, thus spending her entire "break" discussing the best ways to help the survivors.

*

The well-known spiritual teacher Ram Das, came to see Amma in June 2004. He had had a stroke several years earlier, and was brought near the stage in a wheelchair. First, Amma asked a devotee to garland Ram Das since he wasn't able to go up the stairs to Amma in his wheelchair. After some time, however, Amma, in her infinite compassion, got up from the *peetham* (platform/ seat for the Guru) where she was sitting, walked down the stairs and went over to hug Ram Das. As Mother lovingly rubbed his arms and legs, Ram Das sighed blissfully.

Need for a Satguru

Satguru literally means "true master." One who, while still experiencing the bliss of the *Self* (God-consciousness), chooses to come down to the level of ordinary people in order to help them grow spiritually. A Guru means one who removes the darkness of ignorance, a spiritual master/guide.

Several years ago, I asked Amma a question about the necessity of having a Guru. I've occasionally observed less than *dharmic* (righteous) behavior among some devotees who are supposedly trying to live a spiritual life, while I've seen some of the kindest and most compassionate behavior amongst non-devotees who are pursuing a "worldly life."

Consequently, I asked Amma, "Can the millions of people on the planet who are living a compassionate and dharmic life without a Satguru have a chance to find God?"

Mother responded, "It is 10,000 times harder to find God without a Satguru, but if God sees the innocent longing of a person, he can find God. Just going to a Satguru is not enough. You need spiritual maturity to make any progress. There was once a scholar's parrot who had much wisdom, but an immature person ended up buying the bird and eating the parrot. Without maturity, just being with a Satguru is not enough."

Importance of Dispassion

A devotee once told Amma that before coming to the Amritapuri ashram, she felt she had dispassion, but after being in the ashram for a few months, she felt less dispassionate. Amma responded, "Not all the devotees have come to Amritapuri with the goal of self-realization. Some come here drawn by Amma's love or because of setbacks in the world. Very few have come here to attain the goal. At a burial ground, you may feel dispassion but that feeling doesn't stay long. When a person comes out of the cemetery, he or she may think, 'Where is the nearest restaurant?' Dispassion doesn't stay long unless you are fixed on the goal. For example, a man who was traveling to the hill station Ooty, in South India, met a woman and started talking to her. He became so absorbed in their conversation that he completely forgot where he was headed. Only when she left did the man remember his destination.

"We are easily distracted by temptations. Most people are constantly distracted. We always need to have the awareness that the body is like a rented house. We don't know when the landlord will evict us. Without keeping the goal in mind, people live in fear of death. You will face death with a smile on your face if you are aware of the goal. However, it's rare to have such an attitude.

"Some people in the ashram have the *samskara* (latent tendency) of wanting God. That positive tendency tends to bloom in the ashram. Likewise, apple trees grow easily in Kashmir, where the weather is colder, whereas they don't grow properly in Kerala. For those without a spiritual samskara from previous births, it's difficult to thrive in the ashram. With such people, it's like trying to grow apples in Kerala. A lot of effort is needed. The *sadhak* (spiritual seeker) needs protection from external influences.

"Three qualities are needed to grow: patience, enthusiasm, and optimistic faith. A child keeps trying to walk even if he falls down. The child has faith that its mother will help to lift him up should he fall. We need constant remembrance of the goal and the words of the Guru. Instead of wasting time by gossiping, reflect on the teachings and the goal. That gives dispassion. People who gossip are just dumping garbage everywhere. Yet society gives gossips a high place. We should never keep company with gossips. It's okay to say no to gossips.

"One student started smoking due to peer pressure. He began smoking more and more, then he started taking drugs, then he started womanizing. If the student had said no the first time a cigarette was offered to him, his life would have been different.

"Likewise, if we give credence to one bad thought, it can snowball. When snow melts, it becomes a river that is powerful enough to carry a person away. You need to be alert to every thought in the mind. Life is like taking an exam. When the exam is over, that's the end. We have little time left to find God. We shouldn't waste a single moment. Love for the Guru helps the mind focus on God.

"You cannot be attached to anything in the world and at the same time be at peace, because too much attachment to anything builds up a lot of tension in the mind, and this is bound to create pain."

Amma, help us to develop dispassion and stay focused on the goal by observing your perfect example of compassion, selflessness, and dispassion.

Importance of Seva

Amma is the perfect example of selfless service, for she works tirelessly night and day for the spiritual uplift of the world. Amma has stated that action performed with an attitude of selflessness can help us go deeper into meditation. And real meditation will happen only when we have become truly selfless, because it is selflessness that removes thoughts and takes us deep into silence.

Amma is always aware of the selfless service that her children are performing. Many years ago in Amritapuri, Br. Dayamrita noticed that a stack of firewood was infected with ants. So he decided to move and clean all the wood. During the day, a few people came to help, but each one left after a short time. When Amma returned to the ashram later that day, she suddenly stopped at the woodpile and remarked that Dayamrita had had to do the job alone.

An Inspiring Sevak

Rajeshwari, a devotee who passed away in December 2012, lived near the San Ramon ashram. She had been undergoing regular chemotherapy treatments for cancer, and wrote down this experience a few days after her last chemo session in September 2012, when she was very sick for a few days with no energy to move:

> However, I woke up yesterday with more energy than I ever could remember having. How to use it? I decided to head for the ashram and do some bathroom seva. Until a few months ago, I was the bathroom coordinator and just

adored my seva! Who would have thought that cleaning toilets, organizing cleaning supplies, and training volunteers to clean the bathrooms could give me such bliss? But they have. I beam with grace during my time with the bathrooms. Yesterday, when I arrived, just opening the gates to the ashram was tiring. I was moving slowly in the bathrooms. Then I tried to organize the maintenance room. I had to struggle to lift a case of toilet paper. Where is my strength? How can I do my seva? This hit me so hard that I sobbed, and tears spilled down my cheeks. I swept a little instead, and again, just the bending down, breaking down the boxes, and walking with the empty boxes to the front of the temple, everything took so much physical effort that I began to shed tears of sadness because I was unable to perform my seva! I fled the ashram and cried all the way home. Now seva is seva. Seva is not *my* seva, but a gift to Amma. So my tears and sadness, though very real, say more about self-pity than my gift to Amma. Nonetheless, I was inconsolable the rest of the day, bursting into tears at this apparent loss of this blessing (seva) that had been so much a part of life. But today I have energy. And I'm heading back to the ashram to give what I can of myself to Amma through seva, whatever form it may take. If attachment is the cause of all suffering, then even attachment to a particular seva is a suffering. I'm grateful for the tears I've been shedding yesterday and today for this loss, and I need to move on to what I can do.

*

The tour staff works for long hours when Mother is on tour, a challenge that is made more intense by the grueling schedule of travel from city to city, often requiring driving all night long. Some devotees perform seva outside the darshan hall for so many hours that they hardly ever see Amma.

Once, I told Amma at the San Ramon ashram that I felt bad when I saw some devotees sitting in front of her all the time and receiving darshan daily, whereas my seva was helping to park the cars and working with preteens outside the hall, and I rarely saw Amma. I admitted that I was jealous. Amma responded, "Mother is always aware of everyone who is doing seva and is blessing them all the time."

Another ashram resident recently mentioned that whenever she performs seva outside the darshan hall, she experiences Amma's blessings very deeply. She related how, once, when she was standing in the muddy road leading to the temple, doing parking seva during a rainstorm during a November tour, Amma stopped the car she was in and joked about the devotee's funny rain gear.

Sweet Experience

At the end of the long and grueling three-month summer tour in 1995, when Amma visited both the U.S. and Europe, the exhausted tour staff had one day with Amma before her flight back to India. There was no program scheduled that day, and the devotees gathered expectantly in front of the white clapboard house where Amma was staying, on the shore of a beautiful lake outside Stockholm.

Amma suddenly emerged from the house and boarded a rowboat, telling the small group of approximately 20 devotees standing on the sandy shore that she would row each one of them around the lake. The Divine Mother thus propelled each of her children into a state of bliss.

Afterward, the devotees assembled around Amma on a pristine hillside above the lake to meditate. In that bucolic setting, they dove deep into a state of meditative stillness. When the meditation ended, Mother looked slowly into the eyes of each of the devotees. One asked, "Mother, what do you see when you look at the world?"

Amma responded, "When a honeybee looks at a flower, it only sees the honey. Amma only sees the *Self* (Atman, the eternal self; God; one's spiritual essence, not identified with body or mind)."

The devotees then joyfully followed Amma to a field, where they gathered in a circle as she danced. As Mother danced around the circle, she clapped her hands with each devotee. It reminded the devotees of Krishna dancing with the *gopis* (milkmaids) of Vrindavan. When the special satsang with Amma finally ended and she returned to her house, the previously exhausted tour staff were so revitalized that they felt ready for another three-month tour with Amma!

Surprise Encounter

Amma is both the loving Divine Mother hugging her millions of children around the world, and a Guru who disciplines her children for their spiritual growth.

I have noticed that whenever I crave special time with Amma, I'm usually not able to get close to her. However, several years ago, I simply asked Amma to bless a friend of mine who was sad. I expected that she would tell me that her blessings are with my friend. I'm so grateful whenever Amma utters even a sentence to me.

I was pleasantly surprised when she began talking to me for some time about life in the San Ramon ashram. Amma assumed the *bhava* (divine mood) of the Guru discussing the need for discipline, stating that the residents need to follow a strict time-table, attend programs, and complete seva assignments on time.

She emphatically stated that the most important thing in my life was spiritual development, and if I did not focus on it now, I would have to return and strive for spiritual growth in a future life. She also mentioned that one of the problems in the ashram is that the ashram residents are focused on other people's personalities instead of Mother. She stated that in an ashram, people may come and go, but the residents need to focus on the Guru. She also expressed concern about the ashram expenses, and stressed the importance of not wasting any money.

After giving that beautiful discourse, Amma asked me what my opinion was of what she had just said. I didn't know what to say. Was I was going to give my opinion to God about spiritual discipline? Nervously, I managed to mumble a few inane sentences, to which she responded by saying that I wasn't telling her anything new. However, I realized what a boon Amma had given me by talking with me for such a long time.

I had always dreamt of having a long interaction with Amma, and she had fulfilled my greatest desire. After that divine experience, I floated out of the hall in a state of bliss, hopefully a little wiser and definitely more inspired to make sure that I follow Amma's direct guidance.

Need for Shraddha

During one satsang with Amma, she discussed the importance of *shraddha* (awareness, faith):

"We have to understand the nature of the mind. Once the flow of thoughts stops, we can go beyond it. The mind is always jumping unless focused on one thought. Concentration leads us beyond the mind. Once we transcend the mind, we realize it was all a dream. Trying to get rid of thoughts is like trying to get rid of the ocean. We need to use discrimination to see what is real and unreal.

"A boy in a dark room was trying to find his father. He touched a table and thought that's not his father. He touched a lamp and thought that's not his father. Finally, he touched the hand of his father. Likewise, we need to inquire of every thought if it is real.

"Mantra japa is an efficient way to focus the mind. It's like putting a sign up that says 'Post no bills on this wall.' If we remember to chant the mantra, there will be no other messages to put on the mind's wall. It's always beneficial to do *sadhana* (spiritual practices). Eventually we will reach the goal."

I recently asked Amma if she had any suggestions that could help me concentrate because my mind is like a monkey constantly jumping from branch to branch. She responded, "Be aware of everything you are doing. This will help you concentrate. When eating, be aware of what you are eating, when you are swallowing, etc. When taking a shower be aware of washing yourself. Be in the present all the time in awareness."

Talking

Amma has said, "Spirituality can be experienced only in stillness and silence. Energy will be wasted if you speak. Be careful when you utter a word. One's lifespan, health, and vitality are decreased through talking. Talk only when necessary."

*

During the San Ramon retreat in the early 1990s, my seva was cutting vegetables for dinner. I was being my usual unconscious self, talking away about frivolous items, when Mother suddenly walked out onto the deck where I was mindlessly chopping chard. She came up to me, took the knife and vegetables out of my hands, and showed me how to cut the greens properly.

As she rolled the chard into an impeccable snake-like form, I beheld perfection with each chop of the knife. After Amma skillfully cut the greens, she looked directly into my eyes and said, "Mantra, mantra, mantra." Through God's grace, I was fortunate to be taught directly by a great mahatma that even cutting vegetables needs to be done with total concentration, in silence, as a service to God.

Need to Maintain a Timetable

Amma said during one satsang, "If a flight leaves at 5 p.m., you need to arrive at the airport at 3 p.m. Unless you arrive at the right time, you will miss the flight. Likewise, if meditation starts at 5 a.m., you need to be on time."

Through following rules, Amma wants to take her children to eternal freedom. Until the devotees obey the rules, Amma cannot ensure their spiritual progress. We are not opening the door of our heart if we don't obey Amma. Even if you are not feeling well, you should meditate unless you are so sick you must lie in bed.

"Writing a spiritual diary makes you aware. Record the time you spend in meditation, work, sleep, etc. Millions practice cricket to be on the national team. However, only 15 people reach the team. Spiritual attainment is more difficult than winning the gold medal in the Olympics.

"Patience is needed to make spiritual progress. Do your spiritual practices with utmost sincerity and wait patiently. If you are sincere, the results will come."

Amma Teaches Self-Control

Several years ago, Amma was serving lunch in Amritapuri. It was already 2:15 p.m. and many of the devotees had been holding their plate of prasad for 45 minutes, waiting for everyone to be served and for Amma to take the first bite. They were getting really hungry as they inhaled the aromas of the lunch on their plates. The 15th chapter of the Bhagavad Gita and prayers had already been recited and the devotees were expectantly waiting for Amma to put some food in her mouth so that they could finally eat.

However, instead of eating, Amma started talking about how people who come to the ashram from far away aren't given proper accommodation. Finally, at about 2:45 p.m., Amma playfully pretended to take a bite of food, teasing us a little, showing that she knew we were hungry. It was all clearly a test and a lesson to help us let go a little of our attachment to food and to learn self-control.

Finally, she took a bite, allowing us to begin eating. As Amma says, if we can't control our appetite, we cannot develop the inner control to reach the spiritual goal. She says the best way to test our patience is when we're sitting before a plate of food.

Contentment Versus Success

During another satsang, Amma said, "Alexander the Great conquered half the world, but as death approached, he was in a bad mental state. He asked that two holes be put into his coffin and to place his hands outside the coffin so that the world could see that no matter how many nations he had conquered and how much wealth he had accumulated, he left the world empty-handed. Despite his wealth and power, he suffered inside and was never content."

Through Amma's divine wisdom and guidance, millions of devotees throughout the world are able to understand the true purpose of life, which is to grow spiritually. As we reflect on Mother's sage teachings, we will be able to shed the illusions of the world and gain firm grounding in God-consciousness.

Chapter III

Obstacles Help the Devotee Grow Spiritually

"It is not possible to get close to God if there is no sorrow of some kind. Therefore, God will create some kind of difficulties through Mother. Having heated the iron in the fire, the blacksmith beats it. It is not possible to beat it into a shape without heating it up properly.

"The Guru will create obstacles for the disciple. The disciple should overcome all that with intense sadhana. Spirituality is not for idle people. The difficulties of the subtle level are hard compared to the sorrows of the external world. However, there is nothing to fear for one who dedicates everything to a Satguru."

—Amma

Amma Nudges Us Out of Our Nests

According to Swami Ramakrishnananda, "In nature, we find that the mother birds often push their babies out of the nest in order to teach them to fly. Likewise, the spiritual master sometimes gives us difficult experiences in order to help us develop our strength. But just as the mother bird only nudges the baby bird out on its own when she feels confident it is ready, the spiritual master will not put us in a situation we cannot handle. Sometimes, struggles are exactly what we need in our life. If we were allowed to go through our life without any obstacle, we would not be as strong as we could have been."

There's a story about a very obnoxious person living in an ashram who was making everyone angry. When the nasty person left the ashram, the Guru ran after him and offered to pay him thousands of rupees to return to the ashram so that the other devotees could learn the spiritual lessons of forgiveness, surrender, and detachment he was so skillfully teaching them.

Amma Teaches Detachment

Many years ago, Amma appeared quite upset at the way a devotee, Ram, was performing his seva, and criticized him severely. Ram reacted quite defensively and was very disturbed by the scolding because he felt that what Amma was telling him was not his fault and that the problems that had ensued were beyond his control. Finally, he could no longer tolerate the criticism and he stormed off. Later, the translator told Ram that as soon as he had walked away, Amma had told him that she had only said those things to see how Ram would react.

As the years passed, Ram became more detached, and was gradually able to remain calmer when Amma blamed him for things that were not his fault. Seven years after the first incident, when Ram had exhibited so much anger, Amma criticized him for several minutes, telling him in front of everyone what a terrible job he had done. However, this time, Ram just stood there without reacting at all. Amma noted, "Look how much strength of mind he has. He no longer reacts to criticism!"

It's important to remember what a great blessing it is to be disciplined by a mahatma. Amma spends so much of her precious time helping devotees grow spiritually by disciplining them. She disciplines devotees so that they will learn detachment, release their bad tendencies, live a more harmonious life, and ultimately let go of their ego to merge into God-consciousness.

Build the Hut, Tear It Down

There is a well-known story of a Guru who asked his disciple to build a hut, and then demanded that he tear it down. This process was repeated many times, thereby gradually burning away the disciple's *prarabdha karma* (accumulated fruits of past actions from previous lives). Through such *leelas* (divine play), the Guru is teaching the disciple how to develop detachment and surrender, as well as faith in and obedience to the Master, so that the disciple will learn to follow the Guru's instructions, which will bring him or her to the goal of Self-Realization.

The previous two books that I wrote about Amma were approved by Swamiji within months of my submitting them to him. However, in the last eight years, Swamiji has become so busy with huge responsibilities that he often cannot find the time to read the manuscripts devotees submit. So, after I had given Swamiji this book during the 2007 summer tour, he assigned a Western brahmachari who lives in Amritapuri to review it.

Since I didn't tell the reviewer to contact me after reading the manuscript, I didn't find out until the following summer tour that the brahmachari had told Swamiji that in his opinion the book was not up to the mark of my previous books. The brahmachari gave me some helpful suggestions about areas of the book that should be changed, and I then rewrote the book.

During the November tour, I asked Amma how I should proceed. She said that I should ask Swamiji, who then gave me the name of another brahmachari, who lives in India, to review the book. I sent the brahmachari the manuscript by email, but during the year I learned that the brahmachari had not had the time to read the book because of his numerous seva requirements. So during the next summer's U.S. tour, I told Swamini Krishnamrita about what happened and she said that she might be able to use some of the stories for a new book that she was planning on writing. I was becoming more detached about having "my" book printed, and was glad that at least some of the spiritually uplifting stories would be used to inspire the devotees.

However, the following summer I found out that Swamini Krishnamrita had not had time to write a new book. So I went back to Amma again and asked her what should be done. She then told me to ask Swamiji which devotee should review the book. When I asked Swamiji, he said that he didn't know who to ask since several devotees had already read it. Then he told me that he wanted time to think about it and he would let me know later who should read it.

At this point, I was becoming very detached about the book and realized that with his incredibly busy schedule, his "Don't call me, I'll call you" probably meant that he probably might not ever get around to finding someone to review the book. However, on the final day of the last summer program I was attending that year, Swamiji suddenly signaled me and asked me to have a senior brahmachari read the manuscript.

Before I sent the manuscript to the brahmachari, I had a friend of mine, Ram Das, who lives in Amritapuri and is an excellent editor and writer, carefully edit the book for mistakes. I then rewrote the book again, following the hundreds of suggestions my friend had made.

The following year, I emailed the brahmachari the manuscript several times, but for some reason he never received it; perhaps my emails were going into his spam folder. During the November tour, I managed to get his phone number in India, but every time I called, as soon as he answered the phone the call would suddenly be cut off. So I never knew if he received the manuscript.

During the next summer tour, when I told Amma that I had never heard back from the brahmachari about the book, Swamiji said that he had indeed read it, but had recommended the book not be printed. I was surprised and disappointed because after all the careful editing and rewriting I thought it was now in better shape than my previous two books about Amma.

At that point, I really didn't want to have anything more to do with this book. Still, I felt a little sad that the devotees wouldn't get to read the uplifting stories about Amma.

When I was at the Albuquerque program a few weeks later, for some strange reason Swami Purnamritananda saw me and asked me to sit next to him. I casually mentioned the leela of the book, and he asked me to send it to him since he might be able to use some of the stories in a book he was writing. I felt very relieved that one of the senior disciples could use the stories and happy that I was finally finished with this book.

This entire déjà vu scenario reminded me of the movie *Groundhog Day*, wherein a man has to keep reliving the same day again and again until finally he learns his life lessons.

When I saw Amma during the last program I attended during the 2011 U.S. summer tour, I mentioned that Swami Purnamritananda had the manuscript and might use some of the stories in his own book. However, Amma told me to re-edit the book, and that I would then see it from a new perspective. Oy vey!

Then, during the 2012 Summer Tour, Amma again told me to ask Swamiji who should read the book, but at this point Swamiji said that so many people had reviewed the book that he couldn't think of who else to ask. However, at the very end of the tour,

Swamiji asked me to have Br. Satish read the book. Br. Satish is a brilliant editor, and only after receiving his edits did I finally realize what poor condition the book was in, and what a sloppy writer I am. Evidently, I hadn't learned my spiritual lessons yet, so I had to keep building the hut and tearing it down.

I now see, through this leela, that my beloved Guru has taken my egotistical self from attachment to nonattachment, helped me learn patience, and increased my faith in God and Guru. I am very slowly beginning to understand that Amma alone is creating all such leelas to help her children grow spiritually.

Amma Teaches Selflessness

Pavitra, a longtime devotee, learned a significant life lesson several years ago when she was assigned a seva onstage during Devi Bhava. Her duty was simply to hand out tissues to the devotees so that they could wipe their face as they were about to approach Mother for darshan. She was really enjoying the bliss of being able to sit so close to Amma for such a long time. The seva was not demanding so she was able to really enjoy watching Amma as the Divine Mother showered her grace on everyone. She kept thinking how fortunate she was.

Then one of the Indian women who had been assisting Mother came over to Pavitra and told her that Amma wanted her to know that she wasn't doing a good job. Pavitra was stunned. She wondered how she could be doing a bad job when all she had to do was hand out tissues to devotees. Her state of bliss was shattered and she became agitated. Pavitra strained to look at Amma's face for a clue as to what she had done wrong. Then she wondered if she was supposed to be wiping everyone's face before they received darshan, or was she giving tissues in the wrong way, or with the wrong hand? She never figured out why Amma had scolded her.

Amma's criticism remained a nagging doubt in the back of Pavitra's mind for years, yet she didn't want to bother Amma with such an unimportant question. Fortunately, Mother gave her the answer inwardly. One summer during Amma's U.S. tour, Pavitra realized that she wasn't doing a good job because she was completely focused on herself. She was thinking of only how fortunate she was to be so close to Amma, rather than considering how she could truly be of service to the devotees.

The inspiring message has stayed with Pavitra for a long time and keeps coming up again and again whenever she observes how focused she is on her own needs and desires.

In retrospect, it wasn't that Pavitra was doing such a bad job of handing out tissues. It was that Mother wanted her to expand her consciousness by thinking of others, not only at that moment but all the time. Amma gave Pavitra a teaching for life.

Master of Surprise

Although Jews make up less than 3 percent of the North American population, they constitute a larger proportion of Amma's devotees. In the Jewish religion, in which I was also raised, one is taught to ask questions and to be open to different points of view.

Perhaps that is why so many of us have found our way to Amma's lotus feet. Among Amma's numerous Jewish devotees are Ron Gottsegen (one of the founding members of the San Ramon ashram in California and the former administrative director of the AIMS hospital in Kerala) and Swami Paramatmananda. The late Steve Fleischer, who was Amma's North American legal counsel for 20 years, was also a Jewish devotee.

Even though Swami Paramatmananda was from a Jewish family, he never identified with Judaism, and when he moved to India as a young man he heartily embraced Hinduism. Many

Amma playfully putting on a kippah (Jewish skullcap)
as Swamiji and Dayalu joyfully watch

years later in Amritapuri, when he was being initiated into *sanyasa* (monasticism), he performed *tapas* (austerities) for several days. This included shaving his head, fasting, and reciting the traditional Sanskrit prayers.

After the initiation ceremony, Amma introduced the newly initiated monks to the waiting crowd, announcing their new name and saying something about them. When Swami Paramatmananda's turn came, Amma said, "You all know Nealu. From now on, he will be known as Swami Paramatmananda, and he's a Jew!" Needless to say, the swami was surprised-his being Jewish was the last thought in his mind while being ordained into sanyasa.

Giving Prasad and Other Funny Leelas

A few years ago, I was blessed to help coordinate the prasad line. This is the line of devotees whose privilege it is to be next to Amma for a few minutes during the darshan program and hand her the candy and flower petals that she then gives to each of the devotees after embracing them. After several years of coordinating the giving of prasad, I had trained many devotees to be the daily coordinators, and so my job became easier as all I had to do was supervise the coordinators.

By the November 2006 tour, I felt that I could finally relax a little while Amma was giving darshan since by then I had many experienced coordinators who would each take an hour shift coordinating the prasad line and helping put the correct prasad into the prasad giver's hand to give to Amma.

However, on the second day of the San Ramon program, Amma abruptly changed all the rules about giving prasad. She told me that she wanted a new prasad assistant every 10 minutes instead of every hour, and that the devotee who has the timer position (telling the prasad giver when it's time to change) should switch every 15 minutes instead of every hour. She also requested that a chair be put in front of the prasad table for the prasad giver to sit on and that the timer should sit further back.

For the next three hours, the prasad coordinating was in a state of total chaos as the coordinators and I tried to figure out how to create an entirely new system as well as how to train and recruit all the devotees needed to fill the new assistant prasad and timer positions. I realized that I would be ultimately responsible if there was a problem in the new system. So, in my usual calm and centered state (ha ha), I freaked out as I ran around in my perspiration-soaked white shirt, trying to find and train over 30 devotees for the new seva positions that day.

Amma has a way of changing one's job description suddenly, to help us learn how to fulfill our duties with more shraddha. If we can learn to make changes calmly and not become upset by the waves of outer circumstances, we will gain much strength of mind, which can then help us to achieve the goal.

By the end of the program, through Amma's grace, the coordinators and I devised a new plan on how to organize three new lines of devotees involved in the prasad system. By my harried reaction to the prasad changes, I'm evidently still in spiritual pre-school, and I hope that someday I eventually make it to moksha elementary school.

*

On a recent summer tour, a devotee whom I've known for many years, a man named Jonathan who used to attend the San Ramon satsang, came up to me and asked if he could give prasad to Amma. On that day, Amma had requested that only the devotees who do seva in their local satsang group throughout the year be eligible to give prasad. I knew that Jonathan had moved to a mid-size city in California. I asked him if there was a satsang group in his city, and he replied, "Not really much of anything." Someone else came up to me at that moment, and since Jonathan hadn't answered in the affirmative, I didn't sign him up to give prasad.

About an hour later, I noticed that Jonathan was sitting in the prasad line, and when I asked the daily prasad coordinator why he was in the line, I was informed that Jonathan had said that he regularly did seva in his local satsang group. I then angrily proceeded to tell the other prasad coordinators that Jonathan had lied to get in the line, since he had told me there wasn't a local satsang group where he lived. I was very upset that Jonathan had manipulated the system to push his way into the prasad line.

The following day, as I noticed Jonathan receiving darshan from Amma, a dangerous thought arose in my mind: I wanted Amma to know that he had lied to push his way into the prasad line. I then pointed out the scoundrel to another prasad coordinator, warning that day's prasad team to be careful of people who lie to get into the prasad line.

Just then a man approached me and asked if he could join the prasad line. When I explained the requirements for giving prasad, he mentioned that he regularly attended and did seva in a satsang group in the same city where Jonathan lived. *Aha! I've caught Jonathan in his lie,* I thought to myself.

I then asked the devotee if he knew Jonathan. To my utter surprise and embarrassment, the devotee replied that Jonathan was one of the most active members of his local satsang group. I felt ashamed and so humbled when I finally realized that when Jonathan said, "Not much of anything," he hadn't meant there was no satsang group in his city, but that his group wasn't much of anything in comparison to the San Ramon satsang group. I had completely misunderstood and misjudged him.

Later that day, another devotee, Rasya, who had been doing seva near Amma when Jonathan received darshan, told me that Amma smeared sandalwood paste on Jonathan's forehead. I was informed that as Mother was blessing Jonathan, she asked Gita, who stands next to Amma to help with the darshan line, if this was the same son on whose forehead she always puts a lot of sandalwood. Gita responded that it was not Jonathan but Dayalu whom Mother usually smears with a lot of sandalwood.

So at the very moment when I was falsely accusing Jonathan and hoping that Amma would realize that he had lied, she very subtly revealed that there was no difference between Jonathan and myself, and that it was really me who was not speaking the truth. It was another spiritual lesson about the importance of examining the thoughts that arise in the mind.

Amma was also helping me learn that the ego likes to judge others to create separation, ultimately driving us farther away from God. After that humbling experience, I really want to release any negative thoughts about others that arise in my mind, and instead to see the perfection in all.

*

A similar lesson was given to me after I had taken a part-time job working with some other devotees in a company owned by a man I had never met, a devotee named John Broberg. I had heard that he helped to coordinate the satsang group in Santa Barbara, California.

During one of Amma's San Ramon programs, I was explaining to a rather aggressive woman what was required in order to qualify to give prasad. The woman started shouting at me, emphatically stating that she went to school full-time and didn't have time to do seva. She shrieked that her schoolwork was her seva, and that I had no right to deny her the opportunity of serving Mother. When I replied that the seva requirement was a firm rule, the interaction only became more heated, and others seated nearby finally asked us to be quiet.

At that point, I was really grouchy. A man I didn't recognize came up to me and asked if he could give prasad. Still fuming from my previous interaction, I responded in a stern manner, telling him that to qualify to give prasad he had to do have done seva during the year in his local satsang group. The stranger hesitated for some time before answering and I repeated myself in a strong voice, "Do you do seva throughout the year?" After a long pause, the man smiled and calmly stated, "I'm John Broberg." I had just tried to prevent my new boss from giving prasad! Not only did he do seva, he coordinated his local satsang group as well. He was just too humble to say so.

The lessons come so fast in Amma's presence that sometimes it's difficult to absorb them all. The ego likes to limit and judge while the Higher Self sees every soul with an open heart. Hopefully, with Amma's grace, some day I'll be able to let go of the judgmental ego and be in a state of unconditional love toward all beings.

Burning Up Karma

During the first night of a November tour in San Ramon, it was my duty to light the wicks on a tray before the *arati* (a clockwise movement of a lamp lit with burning camphor to propitiate a deity or esteemed guest, usually signifying the closing of a ceremonial worship). Once the wicks were lit, I was to hand the tray to the devotees who would circle the lamp in front of Amma at the end of bhajans. As the blissful, thunderous singing died down and the hall lights dimmed, I began to light the three wicks in the tray with a lighter.

I lit the first two wicks, but as I tried to light the third one, to my dismay it wouldn't light. Since I was sitting on the floor next to the tray, I kept trying to light the wick holding my hand and the lighter in a horizontal position. Every time I flicked the lighter, the flame would burn my thumb. Usually children learn to stay away from a hot stove after the first time they get burned, but I kept repeating my approach, fully expecting my thumb to ignite before the wicks.

The arati music began as the devotees in the hall were wondering why no one was circling the arati tray in front of Amma. As beads of sweat poured down my face, I realized that I didn't care how many times I burned myself if only the wicks would light. Interestingly, many years before I had been asked on several

Amma blessing a devotee performing arati

occasions to attend a fire-walking ceremony where the participant learns to walk over hot coals to transcend one's fears. I always declined to attend such events out of fear that I might get burned.

Finally, after what seemed like an eternity of embarrassment, an Indian woman leaned over and poured a little more oil on the wicks, and suddenly all three wicks were lit. With Amma's grace,

I ended up with only a small burn blister on my thumb that subsided the next day. Now that's what I call burning up karma.

Amma Teaches Compassion

During the beginning of the American tour some years ago, I was working with preteens in Seattle, organizing games in the swimming pool. I had just gotten out of the pool and was resting in a lounge chair, and instead of being in the present moment, my monkey mind began jumping from one distant branch to another.

I had had an ongoing dispute with one ashram resident, Eric, for many years, but recently we had been getting along better. My ego probably didn't like the new amiable relationship with him because my ego tends to identify with conflict to maintain its separate identity. As I sat by the pool, I found myself thinking negative thoughts about Eric. While watching the children play, I suddenly became furious with something Eric had said to me a long time ago.

Obsessing on negative thoughts not only increases the ego's sense of separateness from others, but also keeps us away from God. Amma has said that the past is like a canceled check, but I seem to be constantly reviewing my bounced checks instead of just being in the present moment. The result is more deposits of negative mental karma in my spiritual bank account.

While I was lost in that old, acrimonious reverie, suddenly someone came up to me and said Amma had just called for me to give prasad. The emissary asked me to hurry since Amma wanted me to come right away. I quickly jumped up and ran into the bathroom to change clothes.

As I rushed into the darshan hall, my clothes wet with the chlorinated water from the pool, I thought to myself that this scenario was quite strange since Amma had never before called me to give prasad. And who was sitting next to Amma, giving Prasad, when I arrived? Eric! He was nervous that he would make a mistake and asked for my help, which helped me feel compassion for him instead of anger. This was a perfect example of how Amma knows all our thoughts, as well as how she is always helping us to jump-start our innate feelings of compassion and to put a brake on our anger.

Chapter IV

Amma Helps Heal Emotions

"If you are filled with anger, fear or jealousy, you will be a slave to those emotions. Whatever you think, do, or say will be colored by the negativity within you. How can you be free when you are bound by past regrets and by worries about the future?

"Emotions are like tenants. We have given them a small space to build a hut on our land. Not only do they not care when we ask them to leave, they come to fight with us. We have to work to kick them out. We have to file a case against them in God's court. It is a constant fight. We must continue fighting until we come out victorious.

"The mind creates such an itch when it is full of emotions that you keep on scratching, until finally your whole life becomes a big, pus-infected wound. All that pus needs to be squeezed out of your wound; only then will the wound be healed. It is Amma's duty to treat the wound and squeeze out the pus. That is how Amma shows Her compassion towards you."

– Amma

Dealing with Anger

A devotee asked Amma, "It has been just a year and a half since you gave me my mantra. Many times I start getting angry, but a split second later my mantra comes to me and I'm at peace. Still there are times when I go on automatic pilot. I'm not present and

I become angry. When I'm angry, I'm not aware that I'm a part of all consciousness. Besides chanting the mantra, are there any suggestions that you have to help me reduce my anger?"

Amma responded, "Whenever the mind becomes agitated, there are negative thoughts such as anger and hatred. Try to discriminate and see what's really happening within. Why am I getting angry? What is the root cause? Is the cause in the other person or in me? Keep on asking the question to your own mind, to your own self, and as we go deeper and deeper, we will find that the cause is within us. It's not the outside object or another person that's causing the anger. The source is within.

"The root cause of anger is ego. It's also important to remember that the mantra that we are using is not the only way to reach God and let go of anger; actions such as discrimination are also a mantra, performing actions with a selfless attitude is another mantra, prayer is yet another mantra, chanting the name of God is a mantra, and doing actions with love is also a mantra.

"However, anger basically comes from *vasanas* (latent tendencies to behave in a habitual way). That's why in addition to performing spiritual practices such as meditation and repeating a mantra, we should also read spiritual books, especially the life and teachings of great masters. Contemplation on the teachings of mahatmas is also very important. When we trace the source of any negative thought, we will find that most of the time we are getting angry unnecessarily, without a real problem. There is no real cause for it. When we really search to the root, the source of negative tendencies, we will find the ego disappearing and the negative thoughts disappearing. When we ask the ego the question, 'Who are you? Where do you come from? What is your source?' it disappears. Ask these questions as strongly as

84

you can, as sincerely as you can. 'With whom am I really angry and for what reasons?'

"Another cause of anger may lie in a previous lifetime. In such cases we may not be able to find the cause. The cause may also be due to the fact that we did not receive enough love from our father or mother. Because we haven't received fatherly love or motherly love, we sometimes feel angry. We become obsessed with negative thoughts. Whatever may be the case, when we become angry or when there are too many negative thoughts within us, stop, get up, and walk. Go for a stroll in your backyard or somewhere where nobody will disturb you. That will also help. And when the mind settles down, you can continue your spiritual practices.

"There are layers of thoughts or negative tendencies in our mind. As we go deeper and deeper, as we progress in our spiritual practices, these negative tendencies or these impure thoughts will manifest more and more, so do not get frightened. They manifest only to disappear. It is just like when we clean with a cloth. At first we will see more and more dirt coming out. It is only to disappear that all the dirt is coming out; likewise with the negative thoughts."

Removing Self-Destructive Behavior

As I was eating lunch during one of the programs of a recent summer tour, a young man sitting next to me told me an incredible story of how Amma healed him. He had his first darshan the previous summer, at which time he was addicted to drugs and alcohol. For many years prior to meeting Amma, he had tried to stop his self-destructive behavior, but to no avail. He had attended 12-step programs and seen counselors, yet he was still unable to let go of his addictive behavior.

After his first darshan, he was so deeply touched by Amma's unconditional love for him that he sat down and cried for three hours. Through Amma's grace, the following day he gave up drugs and alcohol, and he has never returned to that destructive lifestyle. He began meditating daily and enrolled in college. Whenever he feels tempted to engage in his old self-destructive behavior patterns, he just thinks of Amma's love, and he's able to persevere with his spiritual life. Such is the power of a great mahatma to help a soul release the worst negative tendencies and to dive into a divine life.

Moving In and Out of My Room

For more than a decade, I have lived in the cottage at the M.A. Center. This cottage is transformed into a childcare center when Amma visits San Ramon. Therefore, approximately every five months, I have to move everything out of my room, which also serves as my office where I do Vedic astrology readings and write books.

Since I have a very sensitive constitution, having a stable, safe space is important to me. I have found these biannual moves very disconcerting, to say the least. More than once, I have become quite upset as important documents have been lost in the process, and occasionally some of my possessions have been damaged. During one tour, all my important possessions, including my computer (which contained the only copy of a new book I was writing), were accidentally removed from a locked room and strewn on the ground on a rainy November night. I became furious.

However, as the years have passed, I feel like I can now complete the move in my sleep, and have more readily accepted the damage that inevitably ensues from hundreds of children visiting my humble abode. Perhaps I have learned to find my security more in Amma's arms rather than depending on my room and possessions for security. I am like a rock with sharp edges that has finally been ground down enough to present at least a modicum of remaining centeredness during my biannual move. My frequent moves are also a great opportunity to learn detachment and to let go of everything that I don't need, so that the only things I hold on to are Mother's precious lotus feet.

Letting Go of Possessions

One afternoon during a recent tour to the San Ramon ashram, I asked Amma the following question: "At my age I don't know how much longer I can keep moving in and out of my room every five months for the tour."

Amma responded quite vehemently: "If you had a family, you would have had to sacrifice a lot more. You have too many possessions. All you need are two pairs of pants, two shirts and some vessels. You are like a two-year-old who has a stuffed animal, and then wants a tricycle, and then wants more and more toys.

"When you get to heaven, it will not matter what possessions you owned, but what you have given to others. Moving every five months for a couple of weeks to make space to help others is nothing. You should be grateful that you live in such a nice spiritual community, where people love you and will help you if you get sick. You write all these books, but yet you still don't get it!"

For some reason, I had a big smile on my face during Amma's response, and I certainly wasn't going to interrupt the Goddess Kali to tell her that I work out of my room and therefore need work-related possessions.

The previous year, when I had asked Amma about possibly moving out of the ashram, she kept stating that at my age it wouldn't be a good idea to move out. So I tried to use her argument about my age to argue my current case in the court of God. After some time, Amma suddenly asked, "Are you like a lawyer who goes to court, swears on a holy book, and then tells lies?" I was surprised by her question, but suddenly Amma's demeanor changed and she said sweetly, "Because Mother knows that you are a sincere spiritual aspirant, Amma is just joking with you." She then playfully touched my cheeks with her hands.

During Swamiji's morning class at the retreat a few days later, he mentioned what Amma had said about my possessions as a teaching point for the retreat participants so they would understand that spiritual seekers should not have so many possessions, adding that they should focus on helping others through selfless service, and be grateful for the spiritually uplifting environment of the M.A. Center. I was enjoying listening to the story, and I assume that Swamiji noticed my smile because he then mentioned, "When Amma answered Dayalu's question, his face had been beaming, and it is still beaming now from her love!"

A few weeks after Amma's talk, I gave away 40 percent of my possessions, and ever since I've found it much easier to move in and out of my room every five months. The ashram residents had heard the story, and I was glad to see that the other residents who had found it frustrating to move out of their rooms biannually were not only less upset, but actually happy to do it, understanding that the move was a way to serve Amma and the devotees.

Dealing with Anger While Doing Seva

Every resident in the San Ramon ashram has to sign up for a certain number of meal shifts each month, which means either cooking dinner or doing dishes. Usually completing a clean-up shift by myself will take about an hour and half. At a recent meal, however, a cook had inadvertently burnt eight large pans. As I scrubbed and scrubbed, I realized that it would take me five to 10 minutes to clean each pan, in addition to scrubbing all the other pots and pans. This would add an hour to the dish shift.

There is a sign posted near the kitchen sink reminding us of the importance of doing the dishes with *shraddha* (awareness) instead of hurrying through a dish shift. The sign also states how important it is to be in the present moment, staying aware of one's actions rather than rushing off to the next activity. However, all I could think of was the huge stack of dirty pans in front of me and how the cook should have been more careful. I felt powerless, and I started becoming really angry. I have noticed that anger arises when I fight reality by thinking that things should be different, rather than accepting everything as God's will.

Another resident came up to me and sweetly asked me to tell her about the most blissful darshan I had ever had with Mother. At first, I grumbled a few words, but as she asked me questions about the experience, I really softened and began to describe the experience enthusiastically. After I calmed down, the resident showed me a piece of paper on which Amma had given specific advice about dealing with anger. She said that it had worked for her, so she wanted to share it with me.

Amma's words were: "When you are in the midst of an up-setting situation, can you simply observe what is happening? Can you stop thinking that someone is insulting and abusing you? Can you forget that you are being treated unfairly and let go of the wish to do something about it? Don't be abusive. Don't react. Try to realize that the real problem is not what is happening, but how you are reacting to it.

"When you see that you are going to react negatively, at this point, pause. Stop talking. Say to your mind, 'No, don't say anything now. You will get a better opportunity to present the whole matter in a more effective way.' But keep quiet for the time being.

"During this pause, try to think of something positive, something elevating, something sweet, something that you consider unforgettable. Try to recall a pleasant event or memory. Focus all your energies, all your thoughts on that. If you can do this, you won't be bothered or angered by the words or actions of the other person."

Healing Disputes

In Amma's bhajan *"Omkara Divya Porule,"* she has written, "If desire is not uprooted, affliction follows, culminating in the utter ruin of anyone in this world." In my ignorance, throughout my life, I have had the desire that people should behave in a way that would satisfy my egoic needs.

I had been having a dispute with a devotee who had previously been a friend of mine. Although I had predicted the disagreement-based on my knowledge of astrology, months before the conflict-the karma nevertheless had to manifest. The disagreement arose when my ego held onto the false belief that the other person should act differently, resulting in my blaming the person.

When I went to ask Amma what to do about the disagreement in November in San Ramon, to my amazement, just as I was asking Amma the question, I noticed that the devotee with whom I was having the conflict was giving prasad to Amma. It's incredible how Amma always arranges these situations. I wanted her answer to be private, but this was obviously not Amma's will. In fact, while Swamiji was translating her answer, he even pointed to the other devotee to illustrate a point.

I think Amma must have made some sort of *sankalpa* (divine resolve), because right after I talked to Amma, all my anger dissipated and my heart melted. Later that day, when I saw the devotee I had been angry with, I spontaneously smiled and said hello, as if we hadn't been involved in an intense dispute. In Amma's presence of unconditional love, it's difficult for the ego to hold on to anger and blame.

I also began to investigate the thoughts that arose in my mind, and realized that everything that I was upset about with the other person was just as true if not truer for me. I understood that because I was hurt, and because I didn't want to see those faults in myself, I created a false story, in order to justify my beliefs that the other person was wrong. I then came to the understanding that everyone is hurting emotionally and that we are all doing the best we can, given our life experiences and knowledge at that time. And we are all learning, growing, and changing through Amma's grace.

In Amma's presence, I was able to release my anger and negativity toward the other person that day, and I realized that I didn't want to believe any negative thoughts that arose in my mind, since they weren't in harmony with the highest truth.

Although I haven't always been successful, and negative emotions have continued to arise, whenever I take responsibility for my behavior and investigate the thoughts in my mind, I am able to release the egoic blame game. I've noticed that when I'm upset with other people, I can always deeply pray to Amma to let her divine love enter my heart, and I have found that by her grace, the energy is transformed from darkness into light.

Forgiveness

Amma has said, "Unless there is true forgiving when we have hurt someone, the wounds continue after death. The suffering we experience now is due to past bad actions. When we get angry, we lose discrimination. By practicing awareness, we gain control of our emotions. If we forgive others, we are protected from the negative emotions of others."

Given everyone's vasanas, it's important to remember that we are all doing the best we can. With this understanding, it's important to forgive others who have hurt us, since we are all children of God. We also have to forgive ourselves for believing the lie that when others hurt us we deserved it, and that we are therefore not worthy of healing and love. Eventually, through Mother's grace, we will all release our negative emotions and realize our Higher Self, which is pure bliss.

*

The following is a sweet prayer that has helped me to forgive others:

Healing Prayer at Bedtime

Divine Mother (or Amma or Lord Jesus, etc.), through the power of Spirit, go back into my memory as I sleep.

Every hurt that has ever been done to me, heal that hurt.

Every hurt that I have ever caused another person, heal that hurt.

All the relationships that have been damaged in my whole life that I am not aware of, heal those relationships.

But Lord, if there is anything that I need to do;

If I need to go to a person because he or she is still suffering from my hand,

Bring to my awareness that person,
I choose to forgive and I ask to be forgiven.
Remove whatever bitterness may be in my heart, Lord, and
fill the empty spaces with your love.

Receiving Amma's Guidance Inwardly

We are so very blessed to have with us a mahatma, to whom we can directly ask questions about how to live a spiritually uplifting life. Frequently, devotees ask Amma questions about their work, relationships, family, health, housing, travel, emotions, and spiritual practices. I always recommend that people ask Amma a question only if they are 100 percent willing to follow her advice.

One devotee who had cancer asked Amma what course of treatment to pursue. Mother told the devotee to follow the doctor's advice to perform surgery and continue with her allopathic treatment. However, the devotee chose not to follow Amma's recommendation; instead, she tried treating the cancer with homeopathy and flower essences. Her condition severely deteriorated, and the devotee again asked Amma for help. Amma replied that the devotee hadn't listened to her advice, so now there was nothing that she could recommend.

Over the years, since the number of people at Amma's programs has increased so much, it has become more difficult to ask Amma a question. Mother repeatedly tells her children that she resides in their heart and encourages the devotees to look within for answers. The conundrum is: how can the devotee know, when they pray to Amma for guidance, if the answer is coming from Amma or from the ego, which may be masquerading as God's voice in an effort to satisfy its desire?

After 27 years of trying to seek inner guidance from Amma, I have recently been trying a new practice to tune into her. As

I repeat the 1,000 names of the Divine Mother and the 108 attributes of Amma, I contemplate on Amma as the embodiment of each quality, which I repeat as I read the English translation of each name after first saying it in Sanskrit. By the end of the archana, I feel more attuned to Amma. I then repeat my mantra, and with each repetition, I try to remember its English translation.

Once I feel deeply attuned to Amma, I slowly pose a question to her inwardly. After that deep preparation, when I hear a clear answer within, I feel that it is coming from Amma.

Of course, it is still important to use your discrimination. One litmus test I use to know whether the response has come from Amma or from my ego is to witness the fruit of the answer. If the response ultimately gives others, as well as myself, inner peace, and lessens the ego's never-ending desires, the guidance surely comes from Amma. However, if the response gives me immediate gratification, yet ultimately results in more stress and tension for myself and others, that's generally a sign that the answer was the ego's attempt to satisfy its desires.

The following incident illustrates the benefits of asking Amma inwardly what to do. When a situation arose wherein an ashram resident frequently didn't wash his dishes, I had told the resident on several occasions that it was important to keep the kitchen clean, to prevent ants from invading the house. One morning, I saw dirty silverware and dishes left unwashed and covered with dried food by the sink. I became so upset that I decided I would teach that resident a lesson by putting the dirty dishes in front of his room. Yet I hesitated to do it, and through Amma's grace, in that instance, I meditated before instantly reacting from my ego.

At the end of my morning sadhana I inwardly asked Amma what I should do. I clearly heard her respond, "The highest path is to wash the dishes for the other person." I then went into the kitchen and washed the dishes, which gave me a beautiful feeling of inner peace. If I had followed my egoic first reaction and put the dishes in front of his door, it would have created more conflict. If we can slow down enough to really commune with Amma and ask for her guidance with the challenging situations we face, our lives will be more peaceful. In this way, we can make step-by-step progress in healing our emotions, and ultimately reach our goal.

What Would Amma Want Me to Do?

If you are not able to tune in inwardly to receive an answer from Amma, you can always do her will by simply asking the question, "What would Amma want me to do?" Her love and compassion can serve as a basic compass for the direction we should take. She would surely want us to be kind and loving toward others, even if another person had behaved in an abusive manner. This does not mean that we should tolerate or condone offensive behavior, but Amma wouldn't want us to react by matching another person's negativity with more negativity of our own.

One of my responsibilities in the ashram has been to help coordinate the guest and karma yoga programs. In the karma yoga program, devotees can stay at the ashram for two weeks to two months, doing seva and diving deeply into Amma's teachings. Recently, there was a misunderstanding with someone who applied to stay at the ashram. The person blamed me for the problem and detailed how incompetent I was. I became very upset, felt a lot of rage toward the person, and found myself wanting to send an email criticizing the other person for her behavior.

I then remembered my parting words to Amma at the end of the recent summer tour, during my last darshan right before this incident. I had asked her to help me do her will with the guest and karma yoga programs. After recalling those words, instead of sending my planned angry email, I contemplated what Amma would want me to do, and I then sent the potential karma yogi a letter apologizing for the misunderstanding and welcoming her to the ashram.

After some time, she sent me a rather curt email simply stating that she had to postpone the visit due to a family emergency. I wrote back telling her how sorry I was about the family emergency and that I would be glad to put her relative on the ashram's healing prayer list. I received an email thanking me for my kindness. The devotee and I both ended up feeling Amma's divine love toward each other, instead of anger, and we hadn't even met in person. If I had responded in my usual egoic, defensive manner, I would have created suffering for the potential karma yogi and myself.

The more I remember to ask the question "What would Amma want me to say or do?" before I speak or act, the more in tune I become with the Divine Mother. The more I speak and act from a space of Amma's unconditional love, the happier I am and the closer I feel to God.

Chapter V

Surrender to the Present Moment

"Bowing down to all of existence is a state of total accep-
tance. You stop fighting with the situations that arise in
your life. You fight and struggle only when you have an
ego, only when you are identified with the body. When
you shake off the shackles of the ego, no more fighting is
possible. You can only accept.

"Where there is surrender, there is love and compassion,
whereas fear results in hatred and enmity. Surrender means
welcoming and accepting everything without the least
feeling of sorrow or disappointment."

—Amma

Releasing the Past, Living in the Present

Mother rarely tells devotees about their past lives. It's very easy to
get caught up in the intriguing *maya* (illusion) of who you were
in a past incarnation. Mother has frequently stated that the past
is like a canceled check and that what's most important is to live
wisely in the present moment.

Nonetheless, some people ask Amma about their past lives.
When one man did so, Mother lovingly patted his back and said,
"It is the present that needs to be solved, not the past. What is
happening now is far more important than what has happened

before. Only by taking care of the present moment will all your questions and problems come to an end.

"It is meaningless to look back and try to find out about your previous lives. It's not important. Everything in your present life is the result of the past. Deal with the present, make the very best of each moment, and everything will be all right.

"You are already carrying a heavy burden. You have a tremendous amount to unload. By learning about your previous lives, you will only add more to your existing burden. Amma could tell you who you were, but she will not do so because it would only harm you. It wouldn't serve any purpose. Amma would never do or say anything that could harm her children. Her purpose is to help you to grow and to open up, not to close down.

"Suppose Amma were to tell you about your past life, who you were, what you were doing and so on; what if you were to discover that some of the people who are with you now, or someone who is very close to you, harmed you in a previous life? It would cause unnecessary turbulence in your mind.

"Amma knows a woman who was told by a psychic that she had been the cause of her husband's death in a previous life. The psychic told her that she had accidentally given her husband the wrong medicine, which had suddenly killed him. Having been told this, she suffered terribly and ended up having a nervous breakdown. So, if this is what the past can do to us, why should we know about it? Of course, there have also been many happy events in the past, but people have a tendency to brood on the painful and depressing incidents, rather than the pleasant ones.

"For a human being to be transformed and to transcend all imperfections and limitations, the past has to die. Everyone has the capacity to do this, provided they have the right determination.

Forget who you were or what you may have done in the past. Focus on what you would like to be, and then, while you are doing whatever is necessary to attain the goal, let go of the future as well. Who or what you may have been until now is of little importance.

"The past can be compared to a graveyard, and it wouldn't be wise to live in such a place, would it? Forget the past. Remember it only when you really need to, but don't settle down in it."

Surrender Brings Us Closer to Amma

Many of the devotees who travel with Mother on tours are role models of Amma's teachings on selfless service. I am in awe at how these devotees work selflessly for Amma, sacrificing their own comforts. However, just spending time in Amma's presence doesn't necessarily mean that a devotee will be automatically spiritually advanced. Amma has said that just being near the Guru doesn't necessarily help you imbibe the divine qualities. A frog living under a beautiful lotus may not even be aware of the flower's beauty or be able to enjoy its fragrance.

I remember an incident in Chicago, where several elderly Indian women were waiting patiently for Amma to arrive to get a glimpse of the *pada puja* ceremony (the ceremonial washing of the Guru's feet). These devotees had waited all year in anticipation of Amma's visit since they are able to see Mother only in Chicago. I noticed that it was difficult for one frail-looking woman in particular to stand for such a long time and I was concerned about her health.

Just before Amma entered the hall, a rather large and aggressive American woman, who for years has followed Amma on the U.S. tour, pushed her way through the crowd and told the elderly women to move out of the way so that she could be right in front of Amma during the pada puja. The short Indian devotees could not see over the large American devotee, and so were unable to observe the pada puja. It seems likely that any benefit the American woman received by seeing the ceremony was more than negated by her rude and insensitive behavior.

One day in Amritapuri, a friend was waiting for Amma to walk by. She had been waiting a long time in the hot sun, hoping to get a glimpse of Amma as she passed. Just as Amma appeared in front of her, a horde of devotees trying to follow Mother accidentally knocked my small friend down, and she ended up lying on the ground with her white sari covered in dirt. Amma stopped, turned around, and helped the shocked devotee get up, and even wiped the dirt off her sari.

Something's very strange about devotees who would behave in such a selfish, impolite manner to get close to the essence of unconditional love and compassion. Amma once stated that she's never deceived when she sees a devotee be rude to others and then *pranam* (bow) in front of her with an angelic smile.

I have also noticed that when I become aggressive in my desire to get closer to Amma, even if I'm successful, I don't have a spiritually uplifting experience. However, when I've surrendered to Amma's will regarding when I'm supposed to be near her, there is usually an opening for me to be close to her.

I realize that when I've become upset at the behavior of a few challenging people, this means I have not learned the important lesson of surrender and detachment. Only when I can see God even in the most challenging people will I be advancing spiritually. May Amma's grace help us to surrender to the present moment and accept everything as coming from God.

*

When I surrender to a challenging situation, I end up not only feeling more peaceful, but frequently receive a boon. As I previously mentioned, many years ago my seva during Amma's visits to San Ramon was helping with parking cars or with the preteens, which meant that I had little opportunity to spend time in the temple with Amma. I had hardly seen Amma for several days when I entered the temple one day wanting to sit near her. However, the crowds were large that day and there was absolutely nowhere to sit near Mother. After some time of searching for a space, I finally surrendered to the situation and started to exit the hall. Just as I was walking out of the hall, someone came running up to me and asked me to do the lap seva position, During this special seva, the devotee would kneel in front of Amma, and help people move toward her lap for darshan.

When I finally realize that it is Amma who is directing the entire show, and surrender to her will, inner peace comes to me like a gentle, cool rain on a hot day.

Chapter VI

Chipping Away at the Ego

"Hard work is needed to make even a small crack in a big, solid ego. Try to point a finger at someone's ego and expose how identified he is with his ego. He will erupt like a volcano, and the lava of protests will start flowing. He reacts out of total identification with his ego. How can people like this realize the truth about their ignorance?

"Everybody craves attention in the modern age, because attention is food for the ego. However, when the ego arises in the disciple, the Guru understands it and immediately corrects him.

"It is often said that factories pollute the air, but there is even a greater poison within the human being, and that is the ego."

— Amma

Amma, the Humble One

Amma is always setting an example for her children by constantly exuding the quality of humility. Watching her in action is the greatest inspiration possible to let go of one's ego, because it is obvious from Amma's every movement that when the ego is gone, infinite Love is all that remains. She has said that the ego, in its ignorance, always wants to be right. That is one of the greatest barriers to one's spiritual growth. Amma has suggested that it's beneficial for one's spiritual growth to apologize even if you think that you did nothing wrong, as a way to develop humility.

Amma, who can speak and understand any language when she wants to, apologized to a small gathering of devotees in Seattle at the beginning of the U.S. tour a few years ago for not being able to speak English. She told the devotees that she only completed the fourth grade, and in India they begin teaching English in the fifth grade. May all of Mother's children follow her divine example of humility, to help us let go of the intransigent ego.

Humble Swamis

One foggy June afternoon, I was waiting for Amma to arrive, in front of the garage at Ron's house (where Amma stays when she visits the San Ramon ashram), after she completed the morning program. As soon as Br. Dayamrita arrived at the house, I noticed that he immediately picked up a broom and began sweeping the garage, so that Amma would not have to walk on any dirt when she exited the car. Upon seeing Br. Dayamrita, who does seva incessantly day and night, sweeping the garage, I was also inspired to begin cleaning the garage. Like Amma, her monastic disciples are examples of humility, who motivate the devotees to become more selfless.

*

On another occasion I was waiting for Amma to arrive at Ron's house after a program. Swamiji almost always sits in the front seat of the car when Mother leaves a program on tour, but on this occasion Amma had asked Ron to sit in the front seat. Swamiji had received a ride earlier, with a devotee who drove him from the temple to Ron's house.

Swamiji, who has the amazingly good karma to spend much of the year in Amma's presence, was also waiting with the assembled devotees for her imminent arrival. Like a child, when Swamiji spotted Amma's car driving up the long, winding driveway, he became quite excited and shouted "Amma's coming" as he ran forward to open the door for her. I was struck by his innocent devotion.

*

In November some years ago, a marathon 18-hour Devi Bhava darshan ended at one in the afternoon. The swamis had just enough time for a few hours of rest before leaving the ashram at 5 p.m. for their flight. How the swamis and the other devotees who constantly travel with Amma keep up such a rigorous schedule can only be attributed to Amma's grace since it's not humanly possible to go nonstop with just a few hours of rest, day after day, for months.

Swami Ramakrishnananda didn't even have time to sleep before leaving for the airport since he had to perform some accounting duties. Swami also hadn't had time to eat since the previous day, so he quickly made himself some *dosas* (Indian-style pancakes) to take on the plane before running out the door. Later, I wished that I could have made the dosas for him. As he quickly exited the kitchen, he actually apologized to me for not having time to wash the frying pan.

Divine Sculptor

Recently, I was looking at some pictures of sculptures created by Michelangelo, the famous Italian Renaissance artist. I was struck by the perfection of each statue and how the great artist could chisel away stone to create such beauty. I have heard that the secret to making such sculptures is that the sculptor simply removes everything that isn't part of the finished product. Likewise, Amma sees the perfect divinity within each of us and she chisels away at our ego until all that is left is our perfect divine Self. When we are in Amma's presence or living in her ashram, we are simply like rocks in a tumbler. Eventually the rough edges of our vasanas will become smooth.

After living for 20 years in Amma's San Ramon ashram, I can testify that this process works. Eventually all of the residents have changed and exhibited more compassionate qualities as Amma's divine chisel chips away our negative tendencies. For example, many years ago there was much dissension during the weekly house meetings, while now there is frequent laughter and a more joyful, lighthearted energy.

It seems like our Michelangelo of the ego, Amma, never misses an opportunity to chisel away at our ubiquitous feeling of self-importance. The "ego must go" for God to enter; "E G O" can stand for "Easing God Out."

Chipping Away at the Ego

Several years ago, I was sitting on the side of the stage during the evening program in San Ramon when I was asked to move the table that Swamiji (who was seated in his usual position on Amma's left) uses for his satsang notes. As I eagerly and quickly ascended the stage to remove the table before bhajans began, a most uncomfortable thought entered my mind: "I hope I don't look stupid in front of Amma and all the devotees by dropping the table."

As the table was covered with a cloth, I didn't know how heavy it would be. I picked up the table with a lot of force, only to discover that the tabletop was detached from the sides and as light as a feather. Suddenly I found myself standing in front of the Divine Mother of the Universe with my back to a thousand devotees, awkwardly clutching the tabletop, which sprang up over my head. I lost my balance and teetered at the edge of the stage, almost falling off backward into the sea of devotees below.

I barely managed to regain my equilibrium, and with the tabletop leading the way, I quickly tried to exit the stage, moving between Swamiji and Swami Amritatmananda. Unbeknown to me, with my lack of shraddha, the tabletop was on a direct collision course toward Swami Amritatmananda's head! Luckily, he saw it and ducked just in the nick of time. I felt like such a fool as I returned to the front of the stage to grab the sides of the table, as some laughter resonated in the hall. That little incident hopefully made a small dent in my hardened ego.

*

But evidently Amma wasn't finished working on Dayalu's big ego. A few days later, I was asked to put a collapsible metal stand on that infamous table, where the evening's speaker would put his satsang notes. Wanting to avoid another embarrassing incident, I carefully and slowly put the stand on the table. Unfortunately, I couldn't figure out how to put the ends of the stand up. As Amma, the evening's presenter, and the devotees patiently waited for my bumbling, mechanically challenged self to get the job done, I became very nervous and told the devotee who was patiently waiting to begin giving his talk, "I'm not sure how this thing works."

Regrettably, I didn't realize that the microphone was on-now everyone was aware of my mechanical ineptitude. As the sweat began pouring down my face and my palms became sticky, I frantically kept trying to put the flaps on the stand up. Through Amma's grace, I finally noticed my hand suddenly move toward a lever that raised the stand up so that the satsang could begin. And another tiny chip of the old ego fell away.

*

Many years ago, as one of the evening satsangs in San Ramon was ending, my big ego began fantasizing about how special it would be if I could give the satsang talk, sitting next to the Holy Mother, sharing my experiences. I suddenly realized that with my sensitive nervous system, it would be a disaster if I ever had to be in the spotlight trying to focus on giving a talk.

All of a sudden, Br. Dayamrita rushed up to Swamiji, who pointed to me. Br. Dayamrita told me that I had to make an announcement at the end of the satsang, that Amma had won the *Yoga Journal*'s "Karma Yogi Award" for 2002. I hastily wrote down the announcement on a piece of crumpled paper towel that I pulled from my pocket. My handwriting usually looks at best like chicken scrawl, and I began to worry that I would not be able to decipher my illegible handwriting. Dayamritaji suddenly exclaimed, "The satsang is over. You need to make the announcement *right now*, before bhajans start," as I was literally pushed onto the stage.

I have never been good with extemporaneous speaking. I was petrified and literally shaking with fear as I walked onto the stage. I must have looked like quite a strange and lost soul as I wandered around, not knowing which microphone to use. After several awkward moments, with the crowd of devotees wondering why I was roaming aimlessly around the stage, I finally pranamed to Amma and sat down next to her to make the announcement. I began reading in a phony, pseudo-centered voice, "*Om Amriteshwaryai Namah*, we have the great pleasure to let our brothers and sisters know that our dear Amma has been honored with yet another award. The *Yoga Journal* magazine has awarded Amma the "Karma Yogi Award" of 2002."

Loud applause followed as Amma threw her hands in the air, as if to humbly ask what all this fuss was about. I continued reading (although by that point I could barely decipher the words since the pen had torn through the paper towel), "As Amma devotees, we all know of her selfless service to humanity. This is an opportunit..."

I suddenly realized that was all that I had written down before I was pushed onto the stage. After a pause that seemed to last forever, with her grace I somehow mumbled, "Opportunity... Um, um, for the rest of the world to see, um, understand Amma's service and compassion. *Om Namah Shivaya.*" As I nervously hurried off the stage, I vowed never to entertain any more egotistical daydreams of speaking to an audience.

*

When my book *The Highly Sensitive Person's Survival Guide* was published, I brought it to Amma and asked her to bless it. As I excitedly approached my beloved Mother with the book, I looked forward to her supportive response, since she was the one who had subtly arranged for the book to be published the previous year.

After Swamiji translated the name of the book, Mother began laughing loudly and shouted in Malayalam. Swamiji translated in a very loud voice, "Mother says that your writing the book is like someone who doesn't know how to swim writing a book on swimming." Amma then made some funny, loud sounds moving her hand back and forth over her mouth, similar to the noises made at the end of the weddings that Amma performs. I was later told that in the Indian tradition it meant that I should be ashamed of myself.

Although I was initially embarrassed by Amma's response, I later realized how it really helped to deflate my ego, as I had believed that "I" actually wrote the book. As long as the thought remained that I was the source of the writing, it would increase my pride and I was creating more negative karma for myself. Because Amma has incarnated to free her children from the cycle of death and rebirth, she will always compassionately help us release the ego. The following day, I told Mother, "How could an ignorant fool like Dayalu possibly write a book? Amma wrote the book."

Mother responded, "Okay, no problem," and proceeded to shower me with divine love through her sweet darshan which put me into a blissful state for some time.

*

Recently, I wrote a third book about sensitive people, entitled *The Strong Sensitive Boy: Help Your Son Become a Happy, Confident Man.* I had asked Amma to bless the new, self-published book since only her grace would help the book sell, and I felt that the book could help many people. Later that day, after finishing my seva, I left the temple through the back exit. Just then something hit me on the head. It turned out that someone had accidentally dropped something from the top of the outside back stairs. "Ouch! What the heck was that?" I exclaimed. I looked down and saw a book lying on the ground. When I picked it up, I saw it was *The Strong Sensitive Boy.* I then looked up and saw a woman and her son on the stairs above, who apologized for having accidentally dropped the book on me. I then started laughing. I felt it was a sign that Amma was truly blessing the book in her unique way, by hitting my ego through my head. There are no accidents around Amma.

That evening as I walked past the bookstore, I noticed that there was just one copy of that book on the bookshelf. When I told the bookstore manager, Kannan, that he needed to restock the book, he responded that he had just put 15 copies on display a few hours earlier. I then told him that Amma had blessed the book earlier in the day and he responded, "No wonder we sold out!"

*

During a recent summer tour, on a perfectly sunny June morning in San Ramon, I was helping supervise the prasad line of devotees, who were waiting to hand Amma a chocolate kiss and a few flower petals. Just then Swamiji told me to make an important announcement immediately. Instantly I jumped up and headed toward the sound system on the stage to make the announcement. However, as I tried to ascend the stage, I mysteriously found myself being pulled back toward a devotee giving prasad to Amma. I again tried to move toward the stage and was strangely again pulled back to the Prasad-giver. This time I thought I heard someone yelling as I was being pulled backwards.

I finally realized that something was caught on my fanny pack and was resting on my lower back. I tried turning around to find out what was stuck, but as I turned around I became more trapped, like an animal caught in a cage. Finally, I realized that the woman who was giving prasad to Amma had somehow gotten her long, dark hair entangled in the zipper of my fanny pack. Every time I tried to pull away, unbeknownst to me, she was being painfully dragged by her hair further away from Amma, while she was trying to put the correct prasad in the hand of the Divine Mother.

I then had an opportunity to practice my hatha yoga, by performing the ultimate spinal twist required to pull her hair out of the zipper, but as I twirled around I heard a scream from the poor lady whose hair was being yanked. I stood by helplessly, unable to extricate myself from this embarrassing situation, feeling like a fool caught in the snare of maya, to the amusement of the devotees sitting nearby. After some time, by Amma's grace, the lingering, ludicrous leela ended, and I was able to free the poor devotee's hair from my zipper. I then proceeded to most humbly make the announcement as Amma taught her son another lesson in humility.

*

Once, when I was doing lap seva, I had another humbling experience. Noticing an old friend, Geoff, in the darshan line, a thought popped into my head: "Wow, this will really impress Geoff, when he comes up to receive darshan and sees me serving my Guru in such a coveted position." However, as soon as my friend knelt down next to Mother, she told me to make sure that the line moved quickly. Since I had already been requesting that the devotees in line should move forward rapidly, I responded, "I know." Mother then sarcastically repeated my words while gazing toward my friend: "I know, I know, I know. I know it all." Mother telling Geoff what a know-it-all I am must have really impressed my friend.

*

During a particularly exasperating lap seva shift on a very hot summer day many years ago, I got to the point that I actually couldn't wait to leave. I couldn't tolerate the intensity and chaos any longer, and I felt like I never wanted to do the lap position again. Finally, Bipin, a very calm and compassionate

Malayalam-speaking man, pranamed to Amma and sat down next to me. I thought to myself, *Thank God, Bipin's here to replace me. I'm out of here!*

I then quickly got up in my Indian shirt, which was soaked with perspiration, and wiped the sweat from my brow with my wet handkerchief. I virtually sprinted toward the door in anticipation of buying a refreshing cold soda and a large chocolate-chip cookie in the snack shop. As I hurried toward the door, I visualized myself lying on the grass in the cool shade enjoying my snacks. Unexpectedly, I heard my name being called. Turning around, I noticed Bipin, Swamiji and Mother all waving me back. *Oh no, what the heck is going on?* I thought to myself.

When I reluctantly returned, Bipin told me that Mother had requested that he sit next to me so that he could translate for Amma about all the mistakes that I was making!

The One Who Dissolves Many Egos

One rather outspoken devotee told Amma during his darshan that he wanted a girlfriend. This particular devotee has a bit of a reputation for sometimes causing a stir. Amma playfully took sandalwood paste and dabbed it on the tip of his nose and cheeks. She then proceeded to put flower petals inside his ears, which made him look like a clown. Then Amma humorously replied, "Now go find a girlfriend."

*

A very competent and devoted disciple named Jay Mishra gave a satsang one night some years ago when Amma was in San Ramon. Before he went on the stage, I noticed that his voice seemed a little scratchy so I gave him some cough drops. Jay has had a vasana, which many devotees and myself also share, of sometimes over-eating delicious food. Amma has asked her children more than once: "How can you reach the goal of Self-Realization if you can't even control your eating habits?" Maybe on the astral plane, the more ice cream we eat, the more enlightened we will become (at least that's my idea of heaven), but unfortunately, on the earth plane we need to control our eating habits to evolve spiritually.

While Jay was giving his talk, he put a cough drop in his mouth. Amma then exclaimed that Jay couldn't stop eating even while giving a talk. She then told all the assembled devotees about how Jay overeats. Amma then proceeded to inform the devotees how Jay had advised one devotee to get an MBA (masters in business administration), as he had done, instead of a medical degree, since in business the devotee would make more money and not have to work as many hours. After the satsang ended, Mother turned to him and asked how he liked that ego-shattering experience, and he replied, "It was great! Give me more!" So the following night, she again discussed Jay's eating habits in front of the devotees. Mother's caring intervention eventually helped Jay get on a strict diet, and he has lost weight.

To someone unfamiliar with Amma, it may seem strange or cruel that Amma would make such seemingly unkind comments before a large audience, but she is only making these remarks to help us shed our hard egos so that we can merge into God-consciousness. Also, if we learn to accept the criticism from Amma with equanimity, and laugh at ourselves instead of defending ourselves, then we can eventually not be affected by the remarks of others and learn detachment. Krishna told Arjuna that we should see praise and blame as the same. Thus, in Amma's form, we have our own Lord Krishna, teaching us this most important spiritual lesson.

Birthday Lessons

In my last book about Amma, *Searching for God, Part II,* I described some of the challenges that I experienced in wanting to be acknowledged on my birthday in the ashram. Even though some of my finagling to obtain positive birthday experiences has been disastrous, the vasana of wanting attention on my birthday has been very strong. Besides my ego wanting to be seen as special, when I was growing up my birthday was probably the only day in the year that I received unconditional love. As Amma frequently points out, we are all suffering from a lack of love and attention, and my birthday had become one day where as an adult I would try to recapture all the missing love and attention from my childhood.

Some years ago, I decided that the only way that I was going to be able to have the birthday party I wanted in the ashram was to buy my own cake and make all the arrangements. To make sure there would be no problem that year, I told several ashram residents that the delicious chocolate cake in the kitchen was for my birthday party, which would occur after the evening bhajans. I meticulously left out birthday candles and carefully designed a large sign that read "Save for Dayalu's birthday celebration after bhajans."

Once the bhajans ended, I decided to wait in the puja room, which is located next to the kitchen, until I heard the other devotees singing "Happy birthday to you…" After pretending to meditate in the puja room, I finally heard my cue of people singing my birthday song. So with a big smile on my face, I slowly entered the kitchen, making my grand entrance with my palms folded. As I entered the kitchen, I expected to be showered with recognition by all the devotees gathered in front of my cake.

115

However, to my chagrin, I noticed a group of devotees standing around "my cake" singing happy birthday to a 13-year-old boy whose birthday was the same day as mine. After the singing died down, the boy's mother began cutting up the cake to distribute to the devotees gathered around the boy. All the devotees were offering the boy best wishes as I quickly grabbed a piece of cake before it was devoured by the other celebrants. I swore I would never try to plan another birthday party for myself in the ashram!

Someday, I hope to imbibe Amma's attitude toward birthdays, which she described several years ago: "Mother doesn't have a birthday. The day the thought 'I was born' dies is the real birthday. That is the end of the ego."

Chapter VII

Amma's Grace

"What is received through the Guru's grace is God's grace.
"Realization is possible only through the eradication of vasanas. The aspirants themselves cannot remove their subtle vasanas. They need the guidance, instruction, and grace of a Satguru.
"Human effort and God's grace are both necessary. Self-effort is man's half and grace is God's half; yet, without His grace, nothing is possible, in spite of efforts put forth."

– Amma

No Need to Visit Other Ashrams

For a long time, I had a desire to visit some unknown ashram, where I would be the only Westerner and the Guru would look like Lord Shiva. In a guidebook on Indian ashrams, I found an ashram in Kerala where the Guru had long, matted hair and looked like the pictures of some of the old Gurus in Paramahansa Yogananda's classic book *Autobiography of a Yogi*. This particular swami discouraged Western visitors, since he said most Westerners were not serious about doing spiritual practices. I thought that ashram sounded like the perfect out-of-the-way place to have a special spiritual experience with an unknown spiritual teacher.

Some years ago, even though I had just spent a blissful month in Amritapuri with Amma, I wanted to satisfy this vasana. A friend and I took a taxi from Trivandrum and traveled several hours north looking for the ashram of the swami with the long, matted hair. However, the driver became lost and continually stopped to ask for directions. Finally, we arrived at a most unusual-looking ashram.

When we alighted from the taxi, we were told by some devotees to leave our sandals in the car. We had to walk barefoot across a graveled, hot parking lot, and then we washed our feet in a tub of murky-looking water before entering the ashram grounds. I wasn't surprised that we were the only Westerners, but I was surprised to see hundreds of Indians walking around in front of an open temple shaped like a giant lotus. The guidebook had described the ashram as very small with less than 50 residents. I suddenly had the strange feeling that we were in the wrong place and I began feeling very uncomfortable. When the devotees there asked us how we found their facility, I responded that it was God's will, since I didn't want to tell them we were really looking for another ashram.

When we arrived at the ashram office, an aggressive man with a long gray beard insisted that we eat lunch. We had just eaten and I was nervous about eating there, so we declined. The people in the office were evidently offended that we wouldn't eat, and the energy in the office became very tense. A disciple then ushered us to another building, where we were told to wait to meet with one of their teachers.

After some time, another disciple dressed in ochre garb took us to a small back room and pontificated for over an hour, talking nonstop of simplistic spiritual truths. When we told him that we were devotees of Amma, he became agitated and told us that his path was the only way to attain *moksha* (liberation). As he kept trying to convert us to his path, I became very anxious and began thinking of methods to get out of there. I finally realized that the only way we were going to get him to stop talking was to announce that we had to leave. I finally interrupted him, emphatically stating that we had to leave immediately. As I stood up, he became angry that I had interrupted his soliloquy.

As we rushed outside, we asked someone where the bathrooms were located, and then the energy suddenly started getting really weird. A glassy-eyed, white-robed man led us barefoot across the rocky grounds to a fenced-in area in the rear of the property that had locks on the gate. The guide then separated my friend and me as he closely escorted me up a flight of stairs. I was told to wait because he had to get the key to unlock the bathroom. I became very nervous, observing the escort's behavior. With all of those thousands of people milling around, I could not believe there was only one bathroom, nor could I believe that they would have it in this locked, fenced-in area.

When the man returned and guided me up another flight of stairs to unlock the "bathroom," I was afraid to enter. I noticed that the room had only one small window that would be too small to crawl out of if I was locked in. Memories of cults like Jim Jones's suicidal group in Guyana flashed across my mind. I was scared, but finally succeeded in using the toilet, and we then left the ashram as soon as possible.

My desire to visit other ashrams ended with this unpleasant episode. Through Amma's grace, I learned an important lesson that day: that visiting other spiritual teachers is like someone searching for water by digging many shallow holes, and never digging deep enough in one place to find the source. Similarly, Amma told me several years ago, when I was interested in performing a new spiritual technique, "The mind is like a bird on a flagpole on a ship. It will fly north, south, east, and west, but will eventually return to the pole. It's best just to repeat your mantra and keep following the spiritual practices Amma has recommended."

The End of Lap Seva

Probably one of the most spiritually uplifting experiences that I've experienced in my life was the opportunity to do the lap seva during Devi Bhava in San Ramon. After being so close to the Divine Mother for some time, I was transported into a blissful state. When the lap seva shift finished, I would sit quietly for a long time in a state of bliss with no chattering thoughts, just feeling waves of joy permeating my entire being. For someone with an obsessive mind, this was a most rare and special gift.

However, in November 2006 Amma ended the lap position. She said the position was no longer needed. I was deeply disappointed that I would no longer be able to have that blissful experience. However, through Amma's infinite grace, in future programs I was able to spend some time standing near the Divine Mother, helping to coordinate the devotees at the prasad table.

I usually get very tired when standing up for a long time. However, being so close to the Goddess, I would remain in a blissful state, full of *shakti* (energy) for many hours. Even at the end of Devi Bhava, my normally sensitive constitution would experience a powerful energy, as if my body's batteries were in a continuous charge mode.

At one point during Devi Bhava, Amma turned to me and said that 945 people were signed up to give prasad. Some time later, she asked me how many people on the list had not yet given prasad. I scrambled to obtain the information, and reported that 200 people had not yet given prasad. She then pointed to the clock (it was exactly 7:35 a.m.) and said, "According to my calculations, everyone on the list should have finished giving prasad by now."

How do you respond to an omniscient Guru whose divine computer is simultaneously aware of everything occurring in the entire universe? I feebly replied, "Many people who are on the list did not show up to give prasad." She then told me to forget about them. I later realized that her indication that she knew the exact moment when all the devotees should have finished giving prasad had deepened my faith in Amma's omniscience.

Amma, the Divine Chauffeur

During one recent summer tour, at the beginning of Devi Bhava in Seattle, I was trying to find a ride to the airport for the following morning. I had previously asked about 20 people if they knew anyone leaving for the airport at 9 a.m. the following morning. I was surprised that I couldn't find a ride at that time, especially since most people returning to Seattle had to drive past the airport. Unfortunately, most people weren't leaving until later in the morning. I started becoming upset, worrying that I would miss my flight. I was so agitated that I couldn't even tune into Amma during Devi Bhava. I decided that I had no choice but to arrange a ride with a shuttle service. However, when I finally called the shuttle service, a recording stated that the office wouldn't open until 9 a.m. the following morning, too late to arrange a ride.

Now it looked like I would miss my plane and be stuck in Seattle. My mind began to spin out of control, and in desperation I decided to sit onstage, where Amma was beautifully adorned in a green sari. Finally, I remembered to pray to Amma for help. Duh, some of us are a little slow. I sat down near the Goddess for about 15 minutes. When I got up, I felt more relaxed and finally surrendered to the situation and accepted that if I didn't get a ride, then it was simply meant to be that way. Just as I was exiting the stage, a man whom I vaguely recognized came up to me and said, "I have a ride for you to the airport." He introduced me to a devotee who was thankful not to have to drive to Seattle alone the next morning, since she would surely be sleepy after the long Devi Bhava. Whenever we pray to Amma, her grace makes itself felt.

I can't believe that after all these years, I still forget to ask the omniscient Amma for help. This leela reminded me of a similar incident that had happened during Devi Bhava in Santa Fe 10 years earlier. By 1 a.m. during Devi Bhava, I was tired and wanted to go to the home where I was staying, but couldn't find a ride. I decided to stand in front of the darshan tent and ask people if they were going into town. The programs in Santa Fe were held at the Amma ashram, which was situated in a rural setting outside of town.

After I had stood there for half an hour, a man agreed to take me to the house where I was staying. Since there was a new moon, it was extremely dark in the rural area where the program was held. After wandering around in the dark parking areas for more than 30 minutes, the man who had volunteered to drive me home began uttering strange comments such as, "It's fine if we never find the car." When I suggested that we try to get a flashlight, he responded in a sardonic manner, "I don't need your nervousness." At that point, I left him and after another 20 minutes finally found my way back to the darshan hall.

It was now after 2 a.m. and I felt really tired, scared, and angry. I finally decided to go for darshan, but while I was in line I kept planning how to arrange a ride home as soon as Amma had blessed me. I became frightened that I had no way to return to the house and I wouldn't be able to get any rest. When I went for darshan, Amma gave me the longest and sweetest darshan of the tour and then in a very loud voice unequivocally stated, "Sit down, now!" while pointing right next to her. I still wanted to look for a ride, but decided I better follow the Guru's instructions, so I immediately sat down. I quickly entered into a deep and tranquil meditative state that lasted for about 30 minutes. The moment I opened my eyes, someone tapped me on the shoulder and asked me if I'd like a ride home, showing me yet another instance of Amma's grace.

In one more déjà vu ride leela, I couldn't get a ride back to Chicago at the end of Devi Bhava in Iowa during summer tour. Since the program in Iowa was only two days long, I started asking for rides the first day to avoid last-minute transportation problems. Unfortunately, most of the devotees were flying out of local airports or had full cars. Remembering what had happened a few months earlier in Seattle, I prayed deeply to Amma and investigated other modes of transportation so that I wouldn't be stuck in rural Iowa at the end of Devi Bhava.

After asking over 60 people for a ride, I surrendered to God's will and inquired about taking a train. Toward the end of Devi Bhava, I made a reservation for the long train ride alone back to Chicago. When Devi Bhava ended, I returned to my room, packed my things and was ready to head to the train station. Just as I exited my room, my cell phone rang and someone asked me if I still needed a ride to Chicago. Amma again arranged the perfect ride for me, coming to my rescue at the very last minute.

What's a Vata to Do?

According to the ancient healing science of Ayurveda, there are three types of constitutions: *vata, pitta,* and *kapha.* Those with a vata constitution can easily become out of balance when exposed to too much stimulation. They may then tire easily, have a weakened immune system, become overwhelmed easily, have sleep challenges, and become more anxious around changes in their lives than those with the pitta or kapha constitutions.

Although some devotees with a sensitive vata constitution may find it challenging at times to attend Amma's programs, because of the overstimulation that the shakti-saturated environment creates, Amma encourages the devotees to go beyond preconceived limitations. Amma is always helping us to go beyond our conditioning, and her grace will help us face any challenging circumstance.

One devotee, who is usually extremely sensitive to noise, told me that when he went on the North Indian Tour, Amma's grace manifested once he started wearing earplugs. Amazingly, the cacophony of noise didn't bother him at all on the tour! Likewise, I didn't think that I could ever live in an ashram, but with faith in Amma, and through her constant grace, I have lived in the San Ramon ashram for the last 20 years. Some devotees are surprised that I can coordinate the intense prasad seva near Amma for up to six or seven hours without a break, but her grace has helped me to transcend my dislike of crowds.

So even if you find large crowds and noise challenging, through self-effort and faith in Amma you can overcome perceived limitations. However, it's also important to be practical if you have a sensitive vata constitution. For example, if I feel overwhelmed in the crowded temple during Devi Bhava, I take a break and meditate outside the darshan hall. Many devotees stay to the end of the evening program, but since I don't function well with little sleep, I generally leave the evening program at the end of bhajans and give myself plenty of time to unwind at night from the stimulation of being in the presence of so many people.

Since the vata constitution needs regularity to thrive, even when I am attending Amma's programs I get up at the same time

Amma blissfully singing bhajans in the crowded San Ramon Temple

every morning, do my archana and meditation, and eat meals on schedule. If I plan ahead and carefully take care of my needs, I can tolerate the stimulation of being in the presence of large, noisy crowds, and can still enjoy plenty of time in Amma's presence.

Being Practical

Amma frequently stresses the need for the devotees to be practical. However, in our longing to be in Amma's physical presence, sometimes we do impractical things. One older devotee went to see Amma at an airport and saw that Amma was on the second floor while she was stuck on the first floor and unable to find a way up. In her desperation, she suddenly started running up a crowded escalator that was moving down, creating mayhem for the airport passengers.

Once, I was driving a car full of devotees from the Seattle retreat at Fort Flagler to catch a ferry to Seattle. Since we all wanted to be on the same ferry as Amma, I began foolishly speeding down a curvy, two-lane highway, and barely avoided an accident.

In my longing to be with Amma, I had bought a ticket to fly to India even though my astrology chart indicated that it was not an auspicious period for travel, and the result was that I ended up canceling the flight at the last minute and losing some money. Nonetheless, I am sure that Amma's grace will always give protection and comfort to the many devotees who innocently strive to overcome obstacles to be in her physical presence.

Experiencing Amma's Bliss Everywhere

If you can't be in Amma's physical presence because of financial considerations or professional or familial responsibilities, you can still experience Amma's divine bliss, for she truly resides in your heart. By concentrating during your daily sadhana, attending retreats presented by the swamis, and attending local satsangs, you will feel Amma's divine presence.

I recently had an opportunity to attend one of the most spiritually uplifting satsangs of my life. It took place by a lush riverbank and waterfall in a magnificent forest in the Sierra Mountains of Northern California. A local Nevada City Amma satsang meets in an awe-inspiring natural environment weekly during the summer months. A beautiful altar to Amma had been constructed on an island in the middle of a stream, under a clear indigo sky, surrounded by immense oak and pine trees that overlooked a turquoise waterfall. The shimmering stream meandering down the lush hillside reminded me of the soul flowing toward the divine source.

As the group of devotees completed chanting the *Sri Lalita Sahasranama*, the 1,000 names of the Divine Mother, it felt as if Mother Nature was responding to our devotion to her. I noticed a yellow butterfly, its wings an intricate design of black dots, delicately land on a bright yellow flower a few inches from me. As we were enthusiastically singing bhajans to the Divine Mother, it seemed as if the towering green trees, the blackberry bushes bursting with berries, the giant gray boulders, the cascading waterfall, the crystal-clear sky, and the rushing, aqua-blue water all became palpable living beings.

Several of the devotees suddenly noticed that the river started rising quickly (something they had never seen happen before) and we all felt that Mother Nature was responding to our love for her. At that moment, I felt as spiritually uplifted as if I had been in Amma's physical presence. Even though I had been tired at the beginning of the hike into the forest after a busy day, by the end of the satsang I was so full of Amma's shakti that I felt like running back to the trailhead.

Through these experiences I have learned that Amma's grace is always with us when we tune into her divine, omnipresent energy, wherever we are.

Amma dancing at the end of a program

Chapter VIII

Focus on the Guru

"Some people have become disillusioned with ashram life because they focus on other people instead of the Guru. It's the nature of an ashram to have people come and go.

"We have little time left to find God. We shouldn't waste a single moment. Love of the Guru helps the mind focus on God.

"Attachment to anything other than the Guru will pull us back spiritually."

– Amma

Only the Guru Can Help Us Grow Spiritually

A few years ago, another ashram resident and I had been trying to help each other grow spiritually by listening and discussing each other's thoughts and feelings about our spiritual lives. However, the devotee later moved out of the ashram. So, when I was on tour with Amma in Chicago, I told her that it was challenging not having that spiritual support anymore. She replied, "You have a distorted view of reality; you're in delusion if you think another person could help you grow spiritually. Only the Guru can help you. You are like someone who needs to undergo eye surgery to remove his cataracts. It's okay to have friends, but you need to focus on the Guru, not on your friends."

Clearly, only the divine ophthalmologist, Amma, can perform the surgery required to remove the cataracts of ignorance so that I can see clearly. A few days later in Iowa, I asked Mother to help this ignorant moth, which kept flying into the fire of maya by focusing on other people instead of the Guru. Amma compassionately responded, "You need to always focus on the Guru, since everyone else is just a beggar looking for love and attention. All relationships with people are transitory. The only one who will always be with you is the Guru."

Later that day, I read Mother's teachings on maya and contemplated her words. "Children, you are all dreaming and you believe that the dream is real. No amount of explanations can make it clear to you. As long as you identify with the dream, things will remain unclear. Wake up and you will realize that you were only dreaming, and then everything will become clearer than the clearest.

"We are caught in the illusion that we will get happiness from the world. Then we madly run here and there, craving to acquire it, resulting in unfulfilled desires, frustration, and anger. However, when we awaken to God-consciousness, we will realize the world to be a dream."

Reading Amma's sage words reminded me of a story she tells. Once a visitor to a mental hospital toured the facility with the head psychiatrist. The visitor saw a man hitting his head against the wall, yelling, "Boopsie, Boopsie, Boopsie." The hospital director explained that his girlfriend, Boopsie, had left him and he was devastated. Then the visitor went to another ward, where he saw another man hitting his head against the wall, also yelling, "Boopsie, Boopsie, Boopsie." The visitor was perplexed and asked the doctor what happened to the second man. The director replied, "He married Boopsie." Likewise, whether we get or don't get what we desire from the world, the results can be similar. Only God can fulfill our soul's longing for inner peace.

*

The following morning at 4 a.m., the special *Guru Purnima* celebration ceremony began. (Guru Purnima means "full moon of the Guru" and commemorates the birthday of Veda Vyasa, the illustrious compiler of the Vedas and other scriptures.) Just as I went for darshan that morning, Swamiji began reading the Guru Purnima message. As I rested in the lap of the Divine Mother, tears of joy streamed down my cheeks as I listened to the synchronicity of Swamiji's words: "Everyone and everything in the world is illusion. The only reality is the Guru." Before I got up, I gazed into Mother's eyes, and time stopped as I entered a moment of blissful eternity.

As I meditated after receiving that eternal darshan, I remembered a verse from a song that Amma sings: "Even your beloved, who said he would always love you, will turn away from your dead body." Everyone who says they will love us forever will leave us, either through separation or death. In the final analysis, all we can do is try to focus on Amma as much as possible, because in reality she is the only one who will be there for us when we leave our bodies and continue our journey in the astral plane.

A Little Help Focusing on Amma

A few weeks later as I was driving, my mind began to obsess about a challenging problem I was experiencing. Frequently, my mind/ ego is so identified with negative emotions such as fear that I have a difficult time letting in the Divine Light. Stopped at a traffic light, I was surprised to notice that the license plate on the car in front of me read "1 Focus."

"Oh yeah, I need to focus on the Guru," I realized, as I started repeating my mantra. However, after a short time I was again lost in my maya when I "coincidentally" noticed that the car in front of me was a Ford model named "Focus." It felt like everywhere I looked, Amma was reminding me to focus on the Guru.

Then I turned into an Arco gas station to fill up, and became frustrated when my credit card didn't work. I tried repeatedly but the malfunctioning mechanism wouldn't accept the card. After fighting reality for several minutes, I finally went into the store and told the attendant that their machine was out of order.

He replied that there was a sign next to the gas pump stating that the machine only took bank debit cards, not credit cards. When I returned to the pump, I finally noticed the sign, and also a small sign next to it saying "Follow the path of least resistance." Even though the tagline was part of an ad for Arco gasoline, the words were prophetic for me at that time. Through shraddha, when I become aware of the subtleties in life, I realize that Amma and God are always present, helping me to return to a state of God-consciousness.

The need to focus on Mother reminds me of an incident that happened in the early 1990s, when Amma helped me through some challenges I was having with my biological mother. When I told Amma how difficult it was dealing with my biological mother, Amma finally responded, "Amma is your Mother for eternity."

I remember tears welling up in my eyes as I contemplated that Mother will always be present for me, throughout eternity. Like the captain of a huge ocean liner, Mother will always compassionately guide her children over the ocean of samsara until we reach the shores of eternal bliss.

∗

When Amma arrived at the San Ramon ashram some years ago, I was blessed to help hand her the plates of the delicious Indian dinner, which she would then distribute to the devotees, one by one. I was then fortunate enough to sit down right next to Amma. So many others crammed in to get close to her that I ended up almost sitting on her sari. As I lifted up a piece of her sari so that I wouldn't sit on it, I said a silent prayer to my Eternal Mother, asking that her forgetful son should always remember to hold on to her no matter what trials and tribulations I go through during this life's journey.

Suddenly I felt something dripping on my head. A devotee who had taken over the job of handing the plates to Amma wasn't aware that she was holding the plates incorrectly and was dripping curry sauce on my head! I tried to get the devotee's attention but she was focused solely on handing Amma the plates. As more and more curry covered my head, I held on to Amma's sari, doing my best to not let it get smeared with curry, and remembering my vow to always hold on to her.

*

Being attached to the Guru, literally or metaphorically, is of utmost importance for our spiritual growth. In one situation many years ago, I noticed that a new devotee was doing the lap position for the first time and was nervously moving around a lot, rather than staying in one place. Amma suddenly took part of her sari and tied it to the devotee's shirt, to make him stay in one place, which helped him focus. This potent symbolic gesture surely helped him become more attached to Amma.

Pitfalls of Worldly Attachment

I recently read a story with an important teaching from Amma: "A sadhak once got a new loincloth. A mouse ate holes in the sadhak's loincloth. So he got a cat to chase away the mouse. He then got a cow to provide milk for the cat. He then employed a woman to take care of the cow. The sadhak became attached to the woman, married her, and had a child, forgetting all about his spiritual practices. The attachment to his loincloth led to his spiritual downfall.

"We need to ask if attachment to a person will help us find God. Be attached to the truth. The person we become attached to will not be with us in the end. We need a lot of practice to achieve this state of mind. Just as it takes years of study to become a doctor, we must practice diligently to be able to witness the thoughts. Offer everything to God. Always focus on the goal and look on the positive side."

Chapter IX

Amma's Protection

"Just as the mother hen protects the little ones under her wings, a perfect master always protects the aspirant."

– Amma

Amma's Protection Is Timeless

Marion Rosen passed away on January 18, 2012, at the age of 97. She was born in Germany to Jewish parents in 1914 and was trained as a young woman in somatic psychology (the relationship between body and mind). In 1939, just before Hitler and the Nazis invaded Poland and closed the borders, Marion requested a visa to leave Germany to go to Sweden. Unfortunately, the Gestapo officer who processed her request remembered her from high school, and didn't like her. The Nazis made her wait a very long time, and in frustration, she suddenly started yelling at them that they should just give her the visa and she'd leave. Although she received the visa, her mother was quite concerned that the Nazis would seek retribution for her screaming at them.

That night, Marion had an ethereal vision. She looked up at the dark, starry sky and saw a lady with dark skin and long, flowing hair who told her not to worry; she would be safe. After that experience, she felt no fear in her attempt to escape the Nazis.

Since she couldn't work in Sweden (where she escaped to), she bought a ticket the following year to travel by ship to New York, where she had been offered a job. However, when she tried to board the ship, she was told that the ticket was invalid. She sat on the dock not knowing what to do. Fortunately, she met another refugee, named Peter, who was in the same predicament, and they both decided to take a boat to Estonia.

Through God's grace, she and Peter made it to Russia where they took the Trans-Siberian railroad to Vladivostok. Although Marion was frequently the only woman on the train, which was full of many Russian soldiers, everyone treated her kindly, and she was never in danger. Marion and Peter then managed to get a boat to Japan, before finally ending up in the Bay Area. During the entire perilous journey she felt protected.

When she arrived in America, she was trained at the famous Mayo Clinic as a physical therapist and subsequently worked in various hospitals. Marion utilized her earlier training in the body-mind connection, and eventually created what is known as the Rosen Method, a powerful tool for reaching the body-mind connection through touch. The Rosen Method is effective in easing chronic tension and its ill effects on the mind and body, and is a valuable technique for finding the path of the heart and soul in one's life, living more fully in the present. There are now hundreds of Rosen practitioners throughout the world.

I have been blessed to have experienced regular sessions from Marion for many years, up until a few days before she had a stroke in December 2011. After each session, I would experience a state of bliss that would last for several hours. It was as if Marion had taken away all my emotional baggage, and I was left with my soul's natural connection to the divine.

During Amma's first tour in the United States in 1987, Marion's daughter, Hari Sudha, took her to see Amma in Berkeley, California. When Amma spoke to Marion at the end of the evening program, Marion was astonished to recognize Amma as the same woman who appeared to her in Nazi Germany in

1939, and told her she would always protect her! Marion told Hari Sudha something remarkable, that Amma had talked to her in Marion's specific dialect of German, confirming that Amma had always been with her.

Divine Lifeguard

When Amma travels for months and is away from the Amritapuri ashram, not only do the ashram residents miss Amma, it seems the ocean that washes up onto the shore near Amritapuri also misses its Mother. One night, Amma came to visit the sea after returning from a long trip. She held out a garland for the sea and exclaimed, "If you want the garland, come and get it." After uttering those words, Lakshmi, Amma's attendant, reported that the sea, like a devotee in the darshan line, appeared in the form of a huge wave, rose up, and took the garland from her hand.

*

Chris, a young man in his 20s, was visiting Amritapuri one September during the nine-day *Ganesha* festival. Ganesha is an elephant-headed deity, and is worshiped as the remover of obstacles. As is customary, at the end of the festival the *murti* (statue) of Ganesha was to be immersed in the ocean, symbolizing the ultimate merging of form into the formless. Chris was asked to help carry the statue into the ocean, although he was a novice ocean swimmer. Earlier that day, Amma had mentioned that the sea was too rough to submerge the murti. However, later in the day, the sea had calmed down, and Amma said that the devotees could proceed with submerging the Ganesha statue in the ocean.

After the murti was submerged, Chris started swimming and was really enjoying the ocean. Another devotee showed him how to catch a wave to safely bodysurf back to shore. Both devotees swam farther out to sea, to try to follow some dolphins they'd spotted. After some time, the other devotee caught a wave, leaving Chris alone very far from the shore. At that point, he tried to catch a wave, but his body was so exhausted from swimming that he didn't even have the strength to lift his arms. Suddenly, a huge wave descended on top of him, knocking him to the ocean floor. As his body was tossed and hurled around at the bottom of the ocean floor, strangely, instead of feeling panic, he totally surrendered to the ocean, feeling detached from his mortal body. A blissful feeling permeated Chris, as if his soul was merging with the ocean, and he heard Amma's voice singing to him.

The next thing he knew, his body was rising to the surface. The devotees on shore thought he might have died; they had watched his limp body bounce around in the ocean as it slowly drifted closer and closer toward the sandy beach. The rocks near the shore scraped his body, leaving a few cuts and bruises, but otherwise he emerged from the water physically sound. The following day, when Chris went for darshan, without conveying to Mother what happened, Amma spontaneously laughed and remarked, "I had to bring you back again!" This was not the first time, it turned out, that Amma had saved Chris's life.

∗

A friend of mine, Nandita, really enjoyed swimming in the ocean and had never experienced any problem in her regular ventures in the sea. However, one day, as she was swimming at a beach resort a few hours from Amma's ashram, a huge wave suddenly pulled her under the water. She became disoriented and the current was so strong that she was unable to swim to shore. For several minutes, she struggled to stay afloat, but wave after wave pushed her back under the water. Finally, she cried out from the depths of her being, "Amma, help me, save me!" Unexpectedly, she felt a powerful surge of energy literally pushing her body out of the water as she landed near the shore. She could only ascribe her miraculous rescue to Amma's protective intervention.

Protection through the *Sri Lalita Sahasranama*

Amma encourages devotees to chant the thousand names of the Divine Mother daily. By reciting the names of the Goddess, the mind becomes calm, the atmosphere gets purified, and the nerves of the body are purified. When we chant the Divine Names, we receive God's protection. In fact, the 266th name is *Om Goptryai Namah*, meaning, "Salutations to the one who protects."

One night several years ago, I was scheduled to fly into the Oakland airport on my way back to the San Ramon ashram, but my flight was delayed, so instead of arriving at 8 p.m. I landed at 11 p.m. I was concerned about taking the BART (the Bay Area train) from Oakland to Castro Valley (10 minutes from the ashram) so late at night since the Oakland station is located in a dangerous neighborhood, and there had been a shooting at that station recently.

As the bus from the airport dropped me off at the train station, I began repeating my mantra rapidly. Unfortunately, when I arrived at the platform, I saw that I had just missed my train and would have to wait 20 minutes for the next one. As I sat down alone on the poorly lit platform with my suitcase, I became nervous as I noticed police cars with sirens blaring speeding by the outdoor station. I decided to turn on the "Thousand Names" on my iPod and began chanting the archana along with Swamiji's booming voice. Suddenly, I noticed five or six big, tough-looking men walking toward me. At that point, I started rapidly shouting

"Aum Parashaktyai Namah! Aum Parashaktyai Namah! Aum Parashaktyai Namah!" which means "Salutations to the Supreme Power." Out of the corner of my eye, I saw the biggest man stop and yell toward the others, "He's crazy." The men turned around as I breathed a sigh of relief and continued loudly repeating the names of the Divine Mother, thanking Amma, for her protection.

Amma Is Present When We Pray to Her Picture

Marilyn, a devotee from Pennsylvania, was scheduled to see Amma in New York during a summer tour. A few days before her trip, she suddenly began suffering intense physical pain due to a pinched nerve in her back. She was in such excruciating pain that she could barely move. She had seen a doctor, who recommended bed rest and a muscle relaxant.

However, the pain continued, and as she lay in bed, she reached over to her night table and picked up her favorite picture of Amma. Staring intently at Amma, who had been photographed in a magnificent gold sari showering rose petals on her children at the end of Devi Bhava, Marilyn began weeping. She cried to the Divine Mother to help alleviate her pain so that she could see Amma in New York.

As Marilyn held the picture in her hand, she suddenly began smelling a rose scent. The same delicious fragrance that Marilyn remembered smelling when she received darshan was now emanating from the photo of Mother. After a few moments, Marilyn began feeling waves of energy coming from the picture and entering her body. Within a short period of time, her agonizing back pain suddenly disappeared. Although some pain returned later, it was bearable, and she was able to see Amma in New York.

Amma Saves Ashram Residents

In *Searching for God, Part I*, I described how Amma saved one ashram resident, Shakti, in a rather dramatic incident. In the mid 1990s, in the early morning of the last day of programs in the Bay Area Amma was pacing back and forth stating that something bad was going to happen to one of her children that day.

The final program at the San Ramon ashram had ended, and the devotees were moving many items in the temple in preparation for traveling to Los Angeles. Shakti climbed an old extension ladder to take down a banner that was hanging from the top of the ceiling, which was about three stories high. The ladder was not completely secure on the slippery floor and unexpectedly slid out from underneath him. Suddenly, he fell 30 feet, landing on his head and arm when he hit the concrete floor far below. One horrified observer remembered literally seeing his head bouncing off the cement. The shocked devotees in the temple came running toward him fearing the worst. A nurse happened to be nearby and was surprised that he was still conscious. He was rushed to the hospital by the paramedics, but miraculously only suffered a broken arm.

Shakti later described the accident as if Amma had put an invisible net beneath him to break the fall. However, karmically, he was still destined to undergo the experience. The Holy Mother later told him that astrologically he was destined to die that day, but through God's grace he had survived. Amma said that the Universal Mother had absorbed that part of his karma, and what would have been certain death became a minor accident. The banner that Shakti was taking down was a symbol of *Sri Chakra,* which represents the Universal Mother. The banner symbolizing

141

the Divine Mother was the last thing he grabbed onto for support as he began plummeting toward the concrete floor.

*

Many years ago another ashram resident, Adam, and I went to Home Depot, the local hardware store, to buy a dozen sheets of plywood. We then loaded the plywood in the back of the ashram truck, perpendicular to the bed. I had my own car there since I had to do some errands in the opposite direction of the ashram.

As I drove away from the store, I suddenly and strangely found myself inexplicably wanting to turn my car around in the opposite direction from where I was headed, which I did and soon saw the ashram truck parked on a side street near the hardware parking lot. At second glance, I discovered Adam pinned underneath all the plywood in the back of the truck. He had tried to straighten the plywood and all the pieces had landed on him. I immediately jumped out of my car and, remembering stories of people who suddenly get a burst of superhuman strength lifting cars to save people, I tried to move all 12 pieces of plywood off Adam at once. However, I found out that I wasn't Krishna lifting Mount Govardhana, but simply Dayalu being unrealistic. Adam desperately yet calmly started repeating, "Please, one at a time." Finally, after removing the sheets of plywood one at a time, Adam was freed.

*

Many years ago on a beautiful spring day, a teenage devotee, Mark, had driven to the hilly San Ramon ashram in his old car. Being an adventurous teenage male, he decided that he needed an interesting adventure that afternoon. Just like mountain climbers who will ascend a mountain because it is there, Mark decided to try to drive up the mountain above Ron's house, which is located up a narrow, winding road. He maneuvered his car up the very steep dirt pathway fairly well and then decided to come down by another route that was off the road.

As Mark descended the mountainside, he began gaining speed, and his car suddenly spun out of control in the mud and skidded toward a cliff with a steep drop-off. He realized that if the car went over the edge he would be finished. As he deeply called out to Amma and pumped the brakes, the car rapidly swerved toward the edge of the precipice. Miraculously, the vehicle came to a complete stop with the front wheels at the very edge of the cliff.

After some time, Mark was able to extricate himself from the battered vehicle, which was precariously perched at the edge of a 200-foot cliff. It took many hours the following day for the car to be slowly winched out of the rugged terrain. This was the fourth incident I'd known of in which devotees escaped injury as cars plunged out of control down the hilly slopes surrounding the M.A. Center. Through Amma's grace, no one was injured in any of those accidents.

*

One of my seva duties in the ashram has been performing tractor work, which I really enjoy, but it can be dangerous. The tractor driver needs to be alert at all times, which is a good opportunity to practice shraddha. In spite of my lack of mechanical ability, I have persevered in performing this seva. One night, during the winter of 2003, I had a dream that I was driving a tractor that was running out of control down a steep hill. Every attempt that I made to stop the tractor was fruitless, and ultimately the tractor crashed into a huge, white wall. I woke up sweating profusely, my heart racing. The dream was very realistic, and upon waking

I remembered that in a few hours I was scheduled to grade the muddy road leading into the ashram. I tried to calm myself down, telling myself that it was only a dream, and that I was safe, since I was only going to be driving the tractor on a flat surface.

That morning when I started the tractor, I totally forgot about the dream. I suddenly saw a friend walking by, whom I needed to speak to, so I quickly jumped off the tractor to catch up with him. After a few moments, I turned around, and to my horror I saw the tractor slowly rolling toward the white barn. I sprinted toward the tractor, quickly mounting it, and slammed on the brakes. The tractor jerked to a stop only a foot before it would have smashed into the white wall. As I breathed a sigh of relief, I suddenly remembered the dream, and felt so grateful for Amma's grace, which had again averted a serious accident.

Forgiving Those Who Harm Others

Many years ago in Amritapuri, a *siddha*, someone with occult powers, came to see Amma. He decided to test Amma, to determine if she was really a spiritual master. When he went for darshan, he made his body heavy as a mountain to see if he could crush her. Amma, in turn, made her body as light as a feather and since a mountain can't crush a feather she was not hurt. Upon realizing that he could not defeat Amma, he prostrated before her.

The siddha had, among his disciples, a married couple, who had been trying unsuccessfully to have a baby for many years. Amma has helped many infertile women have children. When the couple learned about Amma, they went to see her and humbly requested Mother's help in having a baby. Amma gave the woman a banana and asked her to follow special instructions. Within a few months, the woman became pregnant and went to the ashram to tell Amma. Although Amma told the woman to go home directly after darshan, the woman felt she should tell her first teacher, the siddha, about what had happened. When he heard what had happened, he became angry with his former disciple. The nefarious siddha then gave the woman an unusual fruit to eat, and after eating it she immediately had a miscarriage.

The woman then went to Amma and conveyed what had happened. Upon hearing the news, Amma was deeply saddened. The siddha then reaped his bad karma and immediately became very ill, not being able to move for many days. When he was finally ambulatory, he came to see Amma. He begged her for forgiveness for the wicked deed he had performed, and Amma healed him.

This story reminds me of how many years ago, Amma went to the hospital and lovingly fed the dying man who had days earlier tried to kill her with a knife. These stories illustrate Amma's infinite compassion even toward those who try to harm her and others.

Divine Doctor

Tens of thousands of devotees have asked Amma for help to heal either their illness or their loved one's disease. I think that if it is God's will, Amma can and will heal any physical problem. However, even if Mother does not heal us physically, she is always residing in our heart, giving us the emotional and spiritual strength to cope with any illness.

*

Amma rarely intervenes in a person's physical karma. When my dad had a stroke, I told Amma that I felt so sad seeing him lying helpless in a nursing home. Amma responded, "Mother can't interfere with your dad's poor physical condition. He needs to burn off his karma. If Amma intervened, it would upset the laws of nature. However, you can pray. Amma will also pray for your dad."

Likewise, Amma has rarely taken away my physical problems when I've been sick. I now realize that I had to go through that particular karma. However, when she has intervened, it has been truly remarkable.

I hurt my back two months prior to the 1996 tour and had seen a multitude of healers who all told me to do various stretches. Mother, the ultimate divine physician, gave me a specific prescription: "Do not do any stretching or yoga postures; just use herbs and oils, and do not see any more healers. Mother will say a special prayer for the injury." Evidently I had torn a tendon or ligament, so the stretching only aggravated the pain. The X-rays that were evaluated by an orthopedist couldn't detect what Mother's X-ray vision could see.

Throughout the tour, I had asked Mother on three different occasions to help me heal my back, which had been creating a great deal of physical and emotional pain for more than three months. Although she had given me some specific instructions, my back had only improved slightly. In a final desperate attempt, I pleaded at the feet of the Holy Mother for her to help heal me during my last darshan of the U.S. tour in Rhode Island. She responded, "It will get better." I felt a sense of relief knowing that someday I would be pain-free again.

I decided to take a brief nap after receiving Mother's final darshan during Devi Bhava. I woke up at 5 a.m. so that I could spend the last few hours with my beloved Guru before she departed North America. I was so charged with her divine vibrations, in spite of my lack of sleep, that I foolishly helped load the tour truck at the end of the program that morning. Once the truck was packed, I realized the utter stupidity of my carrying heavy items, even though my back felt better. Although I thought that I might have re-injured my back, I hoped that Mother's energy could have nullified the laws of science in this case.

Upon arising the next morning, I was pleasantly surprised to find that my back felt better than it had since the injury. I inwardly said to Amma, "Oh, Mother... joy, joy, joy...you have given me so much joy!" It seems that Amma decides when to heal her children, according to God's divine law.

*

At the Chicago ashram in June 2014, during the U.S. tour, just before Amma came out for Devi Bhava, I was walking down the dimly lit backstairs behind the stage. Suddenly I tripped over some boxes, fell down the flight of stairs, and landed on my ribs. A doctor told me that even if the ribs were broken, there was no treatment other than taking pain medication. He also said that the ribs would hurt for six weeks. After being in severe pain for two days, in Boston, I finally told Amma about my injury. She seemed to look right into the core of my being as she stated emphatically, "Don't lift anything."

When I woke up the next morning, I was expecting more of the same intense pain as I got out of bed. However, I was pleasantly surprised when I realized that I was feeling virtually no pain. In fact, I remained pain-free in the coming weeks. Later, when I looked at my astrological chart, I noticed that the day I told Amma about the injury was one of the best astrological time periods in my life for receiving blessings from the Guru.

*

One night many years ago, I received a call from a devotee friend named Aravind Metaxas, asking me how he could get someone on the ashram prayer list. I was just leaving my room to go to bhajans and told him he was in luck, that I had the information on my computer and had almost deleted it the day before. I casually asked him who needed healing and he responded that his sister, Ariste, and his eleven-year-old niece, Sabena, were traveling in Northern Thailand, and that Sabena had become very ill and been hospitalized.

The doctors gave the girl many tests but couldn't figure out what the problem was, and she was in a great deal of pain. I knew both Aravind's sister and niece, and was distressed to hear of the girl's dismal situation. He said that one of the main problems was that the Thai doctors didn't speak much English, and his relatives were scared at being so isolated. I asked Aravind what hospital Sabena was in. When he responded that she was in Chiang Mai University hospital, I replied that "coincidentally," a Thai foreign exchange student who had lived with me for a year many years before, Tone, with whom I was still in touch, was now a doctor at that Chiang Mai hospital and spoke perfect English. I had brought Tone to see Amma in 1992, and although he hadn't seen her since, he had deep, loving memories of his darshan.

Another "coincidence" was that only a month earlier, an old friend of Tone's had contacted me and given me Tone's new cell phone number. Ariste called Tone, and after consulting with the other doctors he was able to help her understand her daughter's medical situation. Aravind said it was just the comfort that his sister and niece needed: a caring, English-speaking doctor who knew Amma. It felt as if Amma sent Tone to help them during their time of distress. I then received several emails from Tone updating me about Sabena's condition. She dramatically improved the day after Tone intervened in the case, and Tone helped diagnose the disease as dengue fever.

*

Some years ago, one of the swans in the ashram pond was attacked by our annual visitors: migrating geese. The serene-looking pond is actually like a battlefield, with a cast of characters no less formidable than those who assembled at the battlefield of Kurukshetra, the setting of the Bhagavad Gita. Sometimes, when I sprinkle swan food along the shore for our two aviary pets, huge catfish literally jump out of the water to eat the food; the swans then pick the fish up by their fins and throw them back into the water. While the swans are trying to save their food from the fish, the ducks sneak in from another side and steal the food. Sometimes I wonder if the ducks aren't in cahoots with the fish and later

One of the ashram swans

split up the bounty. At times, the swans have attacked goslings, to prevent an invasion of their territory by foreign marauders. In turn, the geese, who apparently view the swans as weapons of mass destruction, initiate a preemptive strike against them before the geese begin nesting. Since the swans' wings were clipped and they are unable to fly, the geese have a definite tactical advantage.

A group of ashram residents devised different strategies to remove the geese from the pond. However, all of our efforts resulted literally, in a wild goose chase, because the geese were determined to lay their golden eggs by the pond in Amma's ashram. One morning, one of our swans was driven into a culvert by the geese. The swan was precariously trapped below the pond near the edge of a waterfall, where the scared animal would have been swept over the edge if she got too close. Another devotee and I climbed down into the culvert, but we couldn't grab the traumatized swan. So we stood in the freezing water between the swan and the waterfall, unsuccessfully trying to rescue her. As the swan kept eluding our capture, we prayed to Amma for help.

Another devotee brought a sheet of plywood, which we put on the dam, making a ramp for the swan to get back up into the pond. Meanwhile, the swan's mate paddled to the edge of the dam where the terror-stricken swan was stuck and, amazingly, began crying, bellowing out heart-wrenching sounds. After some time, Amma answered our prayers, and we were finally able to maneuver the swan back into the pond. Once the swan returned to the pond, the two swans literally began hugging each other as their heads gently met. It was quite touching to witness the tender sight of the swans hugging each other, but, after all, they have been residing in the hugging saint's ashram.

*

In October 2007 the San Ramon ashram acquired two newborn Holstein calves, which Amma later named Amrita Lakshmi and Amrita Sindhu. The residents were charmed by the little calves, whom we daily fed warm milk in very big baby bottles. Triptta, one of the ashram residents, became the main caretaker of our newest residents. Within a year and a half, they were weighing 1,500 pounds!

A few days after Amma left the San Ramon ashram in June 2008, we were having a hot spell, with the temperature often soaring over 100 degrees. One morning, I went to feed the calves and found Amrita Sindhu collapsed. I immediately contacted the only vet for large animals who made "house calls" in the

Amma blessing an ashram calf with Triptta, the main
cow caretaker, and the author joyfully watching

area, but he couldn't come since his truck had broken down. I then called a local dairyman and described Sindhu's symptoms. The cattleman told me that Sindhu would probably die, since she was unable to get up out of the sun. I immediately called Triptta, who was on tour with Amma in Los Angeles and asked her to tell Amma about the dangerous situation. Then I called a local devotee, Richard Morey, who was raised on a cattle ranch. Richard spoke to his dad, who instructed him to give Sindhu a shot of penicillin.

There was a local veterinary clinic near the ashram where we had taken the calves when they were newborns, but he had told us unequivocally that he never made house calls.

The next morning, by Amma's grace, Sindhu was still alive, but not doing well. I called the local vet at 8:30 a.m., and the receptionist said he was busy the entire day, but would try to call back. However, when I didn't hear from him by 11:30, I called the clinic again, to beg the receptionist if I could stop by, to describe the symptoms to the vet and obtain the correct medication. The receptionist put me on hold for a long time, but then amazingly she said that the vet could come to the ashram right now to see the cow, since he had to drive to his house, which was located just past the ashram. The vet quickly diagnosed the problem, gave Sindhu the proper medication, and owing to Amma's divine intervention, she recovered quickly.

*

Larry Pressler, a former U.S. senator who attended Amma's grand 50th birthday celebrations in India, gave a powerful speech during the program. Some devotees wondered what kind of experience he had with Amma. After the birthday, one of the swamis sent an email to Senator Pressler expressing his gratitude for his participation and asking if he enjoyed the program. He responded that when he went for darshan, Amma kept rubbing him on a specific part of his body. He was surprised since he was scheduled to have surgery a few weeks after his trip to India on the exact spot where Amma had compassionately touched him. He later offered to help Mother's charitable activities in any manner that he could.

*

Several years ago a devotee, Amba Allen, was experiencing dizzy spells. Her doctor said that she needed to have a pacemaker installed in her heart. Because the surgery is a common procedure, I wasn't too concerned about it. However, another devotee named Radha, who was at the hospital during the surgery, called me with some frightening news: fluid had begun collecting in Amba's heart after the surgery and had caused serious complications. Amba's condition was dangerous, and I was informed that she would have to be transferred to another hospital for a second surgery, which would consist of making a hole in her heart area to drain the fluid.

I immediately went to the puja room in the San Ramon ashram and, with a few other devotees, we dedicated an archana to Amba. As we were repeating the names of the Divine Mother, I suddenly had a clear vision of Amma sucking the fluid out of Amba's heart with a long straw. About an hour after we completed the archana, I called Radha who informed me that before the doctors were to begin the second procedure, they were surprised to discover that the fluid had strangely disappeared from Amba's heart, and so it was no longer necessary to perform the second surgery. She was sent to her room, where she was resting peacefully.

*

Malathy, a devotee from Northern California, sustained a severe back injury many years ago. Nevertheless, she worked relentlessly during the Summer tour of 2006, which may have contributed to the worsening of her condition. For several months before Amma's visit to San Ramon in 2007, she was in severe pain. Malathy went for darshan one day and winced in pain when she knelt down in front of Amma. Mother also expressed pain at seeing her darling daughter suffering so much. During Amma's embrace, suddenly a wave of deep pain rose from Malathy's lower back up her spine to the top of her head. By the end of the darshan she was pain-free, and the severe back pain has never returned.

*

My son, Dave, and his wife, Sharon, were looking forward to the birth of their new baby in October 2006. At the end of August, Dave called to inform me that Sharon had been admitted to the hospital because of excessive bleeding. I was told that this was not such an extraordinary circumstance for a pregnant woman. However, when she was released from the hospital a few days later, even though she was confined to bed rest, she again suffered severe bleeding. This time the situation became serious, and the doctor told Sharon that her condition was so dangerous that she needed to remain in the hospital until the baby was born.

I immediately emailed a picture of Sharon and Dave to a friend in Amritapuri and asked Amma to please pray for Sharon's health, so that the baby would be born without any complications. I was very surprised and pleased when I heard that Amma had put the picture of Sharon and Dave on her night table and looked at it daily. On the morning of Amma's birthday, September 27th, within minutes of Amma's own birth time, the doctor performed a Caesarian operation on Sharon, and a healthy, five-pound girl, Meaghan, was born. Amma's grace really touched my heart.

For many years, I had wanted all my relatives to receive Amma's darshan and had felt frustrated when some of them were not willing to come. I now realized that my relatives would receive the benefits of my spiritual connection with Amma, regardless of whether they had received her darshan. Recently, Amma told a devotee whose father had committed suicide that she is helping her father's soul by doing her spiritual practices.

*

A devotee who resided in Amritapuri developed severe arthritic pain in her left arm. It created so much discomfort that she couldn't even have clothes cover her arm. She was going through a very difficult astrological period but didn't want to bother Amma by telling her about the severity of her physical condition. However, during Devi Bhava, the girl's father asked Amma to help his daughter with her unbearable physical situation. Within minutes of Amma hearing about the condition, the devotee's pain suddenly and permanently disappeared, after six months of severe agony.

*

The coordinators of the Sante Fe ashram, Steve and Amritapriya Schmidt, decided to go for a horseback ride one winter morning during January 1993. They had just returned from spending Christmas in Amritapuri. Amritapriya had purchased a new horse, which had been represented by the seller as a gentle animal, suitable even for a child to ride. Steve was riding the new horse for the first time that day, and from the beginning of the ride the horse seemed excited and was difficult to control.

As they were finishing the ride, following a road that went steeply downhill, Steve's horse suddenly bolted out of control, and he flew out of the saddle, landing with incredible force on his face on the rocky road. It was an incredibly hard fall!

Steve's first thought was that he must be dead, but he realized that it couldn't be true because he could hear Amritapriya's voice. Then he thought that he must have broken his neck, or back, or perhaps damaged his brain. As he slowly began moving his head and limbs, he discovered that everything seemed to be in working order. He suddenly had a strong sense of Amma's presence. As he remembered flying through the air and crashing to the ground, he realized something was very unusual. He had not felt the landing on the hard road, but felt instead as if he had landed in Amma's arms.

Bruised, sore, and dazed, he was brought to the emergency room. At the hospital the doctors took several scans. Steve was told that he had a bruised spinal cord in the neck area, which could have resulted in paralysis. He was also told that because his spinal canal was narrower than average, it was a miracle that he had not sustained a serious permanent injury.

He stayed in the hospital overnight and was released the next day. Steve's face was black and blue and covered with lacerations, and his hands continued to sting painfully at times as a result of the bruised spinal cord, but there were no serious long-term injuries.

When Steve returned from the hospital, he noticed a profound feeling of well-being and bliss spreading over him. His mind was very still and peaceful, without the usual stream of incessant thoughts. He was having joyful, focused meditations as his mind quieted down. Steve's heart was so open that when he would talk to someone, he would frequently start crying. He thought, "This is what a human being should feel like, having all this love."

Steve sent Amma a letter telling her about the accident and thanking her for her grace. He felt that she had been with him at the time of the accident, and the image of falling into her arms as he flew through the air remained vividly with him. Mother sent a beautiful letter to Steve stating, "The extent of the injury was greatly reduced." As Steve read Amma's letter, he was deeply moved: it confirmed his feeling that Amma had saved him from serious harm.

A few months later, during Amma's summer tour in the U.S., one of Amma's swamis told Steve that one day he had been in Amma's room when she suddenly exclaimed, "My child has just been in an accident! I have to help!" At that time, the swami had no idea what Amma was talking about, but later, when Steve's letter about the accident arrived, the swami understood that Mother was referring to Steve, because the accident and Amma's comment occurred at the same time. When Steve heard this story, he began sobbing as he realized Mother's incredible compassion for her children.

Later during the summer tour, Steve was still having one residual effect from the accident. His hands were swollen, red, and painful. He felt that after all Amma had done for him, he couldn't ask her for anything more. However, during his Devi Bhava darshan, he mentally asked her to send a little energy toward his hands. Mother immediately reached for his hands and started rubbing flowers on them. Afterward, the pain and swelling in his hands completely disappeared.

Later, Steve discovered that the man who had sold him the horse had lied, putting him and Amritapriya in danger in order to sell a difficult horse quickly. However, instead of being angry with the man, he felt grateful, since the experience ultimately gave him such an amazing and deep experience with Amma. The experience really deepened Steve's faith in Amma, for he had clearly been saved from a permanent, disabling injury by her grace. Steve felt that it was one thing to know intellectually that Amma is an omniscient mahatma, and altogether different to learn that she had known of his accident halfway around the world, in the moment it occurred. He then came upon this poignant quote by Amma: "Faith is to believe something which you feel. This something is not visible or tangible. It is an experience. Just like love, faith, too, is an experience. The experience of faith is personal and subjective. When one is endowed with faith, one knows through one's own experience, and nothing needs to be proven."

*

Aravind, a devotee from San Diego, survived a traumatic experience, thanks to Amma's grace. He was taking a shower one sunny July afternoon in San Diego when he suddenly began experiencing severe pain in his chest. He collapsed to the bathroom floor, writhing in pain. Just at that moment a friend who was on tour with Amma "just happened" to call him from Chicago. He was barely able to crawl over to answer the phone. Aravind described what was happening and his friend advised him to call 911 immediately.

Aravind called 911, but before he could complete the call, he abruptly became unconscious. The paramedics were able to trace the call and rushed to his house, where they found him lying unconscious on the bathroom floor. Just as the paramedics were leaving the house Aravind's cell phone rang, and the paramedics explained the situation to his friend in Chicago.

When Aravind was taken to the emergency room, the doctors treated him for a heart attack and gave him blood thinners, which only worsened his condition. The aorta in his heart had burst, and he lost a lot of blood. Once the doctors had correctly diagnosed his condition, they immediately performed open-heart surgery to patch the aorta. However, his heart had stopped beating for 30 minutes, and the attending physicians declared him dead.

When his friend in Chicago called the hospital for an update on Aravind's condition, she was sadly informed that he had just died. The distraught devotee ran into the hall, where Amma was giving darshan, and with tears rolling down her face told Amma what had just happened. Amma waited some time and then responded, "Don't worry, he'll be okay."

Within minutes of Amma's comment, Aravind's heart suddenly began beating. However, even though he was now alive, the doctors said that his chances for survival were dismal. Aravind's family and friends had to encourage the doctors not to give up. A few hours later, a neurosurgeon read the X-rays and scans of his brain and stated that all the black spots indicated that even if he survived, he would be in a vegetative state for the rest of his life.

When Aravind finally regained consciousness five days later, he quickly proved the neurosurgeons wrong. He said that he felt like a newborn baby floating in a sea of bliss. He later joked that his aorta bursting was really the ultimate heart-opening experience. However, his entire left side was paralyzed, and he had been given 13 units of blood, indicating that he had lost most of the blood in his body. After remaining in the hospital for two months, he began an arduous program of physical therapy. He had to learn how to walk and speak again. By Amma's grace, the recovery went quicker than the doctors expected.

Approximately eight months after the incident, Aravind needed to have another surgery to replace his aorta and one of the other heart valves, since he couldn't continue living with the patched aorta and damaged valve. A few days before the surgery, Amma talked to him on the phone from India and asked him how he was feeling. She ended the conversation by saying, "Don't worry, everything will be okay. Surgery, no problem." She lovingly sent him a kiss via the phone.

The second surgery was completed without any complication. When he was in the intensive care unit after the surgery, Aravind had placed several large pictures of Amma in his room. "Coincidentally," both his nurses in the hospital had previously received Amma's darshan. Amma takes such loving care of her devotees.

*

As I previously mentioned, Amma will only intervene and heal our bodies if it is God's will. However, even if she doesn't heal us, her compassionate love will help us cope with our karma. Amma's only American swami, Swami Paramatmananda, who is now serving at the AIMS hospital (Amma's high-tech, specialty hospital in Cochin, India), has had numerous, serious health challenges for many years. Amma told him that if she healed him, he might have to be reborn again, but if he continues to bear his physical karma he might be liberated, and if so, his soul will forever merge with God after this lifetime.

As difficult as it has been for Swami Paramatmananda to cope with his many physical challenges, his dedication to reaching the goal has been an inspiration to all of Amma's devotees. His sense of humor in dealing with his illnesses has also been an inspiration. I fondly remember his reaction to some pain he was experiencing: "Get a body, get a problem. No body, no problem!"

*

Ron Gottsegen helped establish the San Ramon ashram in California, and was also the founding administrator of the AIMS hospital. Like many of Amma's senior devotees, he has often worked 16 hours a day, seven days a week, forgoing sleep and food at times to complete Amma's work. He has also suffered from a sore back from sitting for so many hours in front of a computer. Ron's dedication to Amma's service has been amazing. I have periodically given Ron back rubs and shown him various stretching exercises to help mollify his back pain. However, no matter how sore his back was, he would always continue performing his seva for Amma. Whenever I asked him if he was taking breaks to stretch, he would respond that he knew he should, but he got so engrossed in his seva that he simply forgot his own needs.

In 2005, Ron developed a rare blood disease that severely affected his health. During his illness, he was convalescing in the San Ramon ashram. Whenever his energy was strong, he would still perform seva, by doing computer work from his bed. As Ron's health deteriorated during Amma's November 2006 tour, Amma compassionately showered her divine love on him. Before Mother left the ashram, she caressed his body while he sat in a wheelchair. At one point, she sat on the floor, rubbing his legs, and, with tears welling up in her eyes, she told the other ashram residents, "Pray for Ron."

During several live, interactive Web telecasts from Amritapuri to the San Ramon ashram, Amma asked Ron how he was feeling. Ron's face lit up as he responded, "Now that I see Amma, I feel fine." As the Divine Mother and her ailing son stared at each other with love from different sides of the planet, one could feel that Amma's infinite compassion would surely transport Ron to a state of eternal peace, regardless of his physical condition.

Ron's physical condition began improving in February 2007. Through Amma's grace, he was feeling so well that at her request he made several trips to India, to continue his work at the AIMS hospital. He continues to do a great deal of seva at the various ashrams in America.

Amma answering a devotee's question

Chapter X

There Is No Death

"This is only a rented body. At some point, we will be asked to leave it. Then we must go out. Before we leave, that which is eternal should be gained while residing in this body. If we have a house of our own, we can happily move out when we are asked to vacate this rented one. Then we can live in the eternal house of God.

"The pain of death is caused by the thought that death is going to destroy everything that you have—all that you are attached to and everything to which you cling. That clinging causes the pain. If only you can let go of all your attachments, then the pain of death will turn into an experience of bliss.

"Death is not complete annihilation. It is a pause. It is like pressing the pause button on a tape recorder in the middle of a song. Sooner or later, when pressed again, the pause button is released and the song continues."

– Amma

Amma Describes the Soul Leaving the Body

Swami Ramakrishnananda eloquently describes Mother's teachings about death and rebirth in his book *The Secret of Inner Peace*: "Amma says that when the body perishes, our soul remains intact, just as electricity lives on even after the light bulb breaks. There is a subtle aura surrounding our body; just as a tape recorder records everything we say, our aura records all our thoughts, words and

163

actions while we are alive. After death, that aura enters the atmosphere in the shape of a balloon along with the *jiva* (individual soul). It then rises in the atmosphere like the smoke of a cigarette.

"Those souls who have realized the Self merge into the Infinite at the time of death, like a drop of water merging into the ocean, or like a balloon bursting, the air inside becomes one with the totality. There is no rebirth for such a soul."

Innocent Like a Child

I was visiting some friends in Santa Cruz, a beach town on the California coast, on a sunny April afternoon in 2014. As I was walking down the street to meet my friends, a joyful-looking woman and her smiling little boy approached me. The peaceful-looking stranger inquired, "Excuse me, sir, do you know where we can get some ice cream around here?" I told her that I was not from Santa Cruz, but that there was probably an ice cream parlor nearby on the town's main street, which I pointed out to them. The little boy began skipping as he held his loving mother's hand, and they strolled off in search of the ice cream parlor. Tears welled up in my eyes and a deep joy arose within me as I watched the innocent child skipping down the sidewalk and holding his mother's hand. As I basked in the mother and son's deep love and joy, I suddenly had the image of leaving my body and Amma taking my hand as I merrily skipped along, having faith that she would guide me to the eternal parlor of divine bliss in God.

Amma's Grace Helps Devotees
When They Leave the Body

In the *Sri Lalita Sahasranama*, mantra 851 is "Salutations to Her who gives peace and repose to those afflicted with birth, old age, and death." Our beloved Amma gives peace to the devotees as they make their transition from the earthly plane to the astral plane.

Many years ago, Ottur Namboodirippad, the illustrious composer of Amma's *Ashtottaram* (108 attributes of Amma), was on his deathbed in Amritapuri. Throughout the day, he kept calling out for Amma to come as he lay in severe pain, close to death. However, even after Amma was informed about the gravity of the situation, she surprisingly did not come to his room to comfort him. Some of the ashram residents could not understand why she wouldn't come to console the dying man.

Finally, the man left his body with a cry for Amma on his lips. A few minutes later, Amma came into his room and lovingly caressed his forehead, confirming that he had passed away. Later, some disciples asked Amma why she hadn't come to comfort the dying disciple. She explained that she wanted the devotee to leave his body while crying out to God. If she had come to comfort him, his desire to see her would have been fulfilled, and in his last breath his mind might have wandered to some other desire. As it was, she said, his dying cry for Amma had carried him all the way to liberation.

*

The first Western renunciant from the Amritapuri ashram to pass away was Brahmacharini Nirmalamrita, who died in 1999, after spending more than 10 years living in Amritapuri and traveling with Amma around the world. Amma had given her the yellow robes of a renunciant in 1997. This very kind, tall, dark-haired woman always had a supportive word and a loving smile for everyone.

She had returned to the M.A. Center from Amritapuri in March 1999, to help prepare for the retreats during the Summer Tour. The ashram residents were deeply upset and concerned when suddenly Bri. Nirmalamrita was rushed to the hospital one night. She had had cancer as a young person, but was in full remission, and had been healthy and strong since she met Amma 12 years earlier.

Unfortunately, the dormant cancer had now reappeared and rapidly spread to many areas of her body. The ashram residents performed continuous archana and intensely prayed for her. A few weeks later, as she lay dying in a hospital in Oakland, Mother consoled her by calling from India and gently saying, "Darling daughter, take my hand and I will lead you into the garden."

I was initially very saddened and surprised that Mother didn't miraculously intervene to save Bri. Nirmalamrita's life. However, at that time I didn't realize that Amma can only intervene if it is God's will and if a soul's purpose on Earth has not yet been completed. After Bri. Nirmalamrita passed away, Amma mentioned that she could now feel her presence more strongly than when she was in the body.

Amma once told a devotee who was close to passing on that he had more work to do, and miraculously he recovered. In another situation, when a devotee died suddenly in an accident, Mother asked, "How much longer could I have kept him alive?" implying that she already extended his life as much as she possibly could.

*

A devotee in the Bay Area was dying, and Br. Dayamrita returned from a long tour in time to see him. The devotee, Harry, was still conscious at times as he lay on his deathbed. With Amma's grace, Harry had surrendered to the reality that it was time for him to leave his body.

Harry spoke sporadically to Br. Dayamrita for about an hour. He said that he wanted Amma to know that he was ready to leave his body. He also told Br. Dayamrita that he would miss the bhajans at the M.A. Center. Dayamritaji's comforting reply was that there would be better bhajans where he was going. When Br. Dayamrita left the room, Harry fell into a deep sleep and passed away a few hours later as the devotees chanted the *Sri Lalita Sahasranama*. The devotees who were present as Harry passed on said that Amma's presence was palpable in the room.

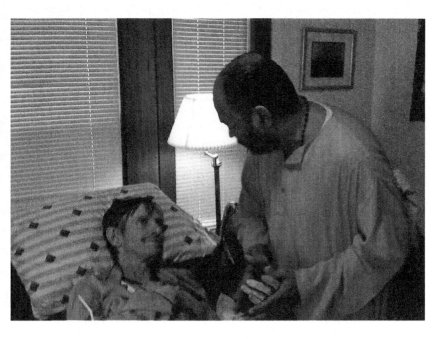

Br. Dayamrita compassionately giving solace to Harry

*

Devananda, the renowned Japanese healer who has healed many devotees through Amma's grace, suffered complications following heart surgery in September 2007. Devananda's physical condition deteriorated, and at the end of the following week, exactly on the auspicious day of Amma's birthday, the great healer made his transition. Later, several of the ashram astrologers looked at his astrological chart to analyze the moment of his transition, and we were awestruck at what an incredibly auspicious moment it was when he left his body. The timing indicated his soul would likely reach the highest level of the astral plane.

*

My closest companion for 31 years, Nandita, was diagnosed with cancer in May 2014. For the last 16 years she spent winters in Amritapuri and lived in the Bay Area, near the San Ramon ashram, the rest of the year. Nandita had such a strong will to focus on her spiritual growth, she only read books about Amma and other spiritual books. She meditated deeply on Amma and God daily.

Nandita was a quiet person who preferred to remain in the background and never asked Amma any questions. However, when I told Amma in July during the New York programs that the cancer had spread to her lungs, Amma called Nandita on the phone and gave her the sweetest and most loving phone darshan. Amma is aware of and helping all her children regardless of the amount of interpersonal interaction that a devotee has with her.

Nandita's oncologist told us in October that she would likely live only another year, since the cervical cancer had spread to other organs in her body. Even though the prognosis was poor, through

Amma's grace, amazingly she had virtually no symptoms through the beginning of December and thoroughly enjoyed her birthday and Thanksgiving dinner at the end of November. However, about a week before Christmas she suddenly developed some serious symptoms, though she still felt well enough to spend Christmas week at a spiritual community in the mountains. The day before Christmas Eve she developed a lot of pain and was admitted to the local hospital. Remarkably, Christmas Eve morning she felt better and asked to check out of the hospital since she didn't want to miss a spiritual event that evening. However, after lunch she started developing more pain and when I called the hospital Christmas Eve the nurse told me that Nandita was deteriorating rapidly, and a few hours later she went into kidney failure.

I was on overload after talking on the phone for hours to the hospital nurses and doctors, so I turned my phone off at midnight after having said my final goodbye to Nandita. I then had a dream of walking down a corridor with Nandita, explaining that she was going into the light and told her to go to Amma, go into the light. She began walking ahead of me and then I suddenly woke up at 1:15 a.m., which I found out the next morning was the time she passed away. When Amma found out that Nandita went into kidney failure she tried to call her from Amritapuri, but alas, Nandita deteriorated so rapidly she had already passed away.

When I meditated in the puja room in the main house on Christmas day, with a picture of Nandita next to a picture of Amma, I saw her clearly in my mind's eye, as if she were literally right in front of me, bouncing up and down on a fountain of light with arms outstretched, shouting "Yippee!"

Nandita told many of her friends before she passed that she had no fear of death and was ready to go on to the next stage. She made it clear that she didn't want to lie around helplessly in pain for a year, waiting to die. Amma's grace took her to her next stage so quickly and effortlessly, since she only began getting serious symptoms the last week of her life.

*

Steve Fleisher, a very close devotee of Amma who served both on the board of directors of the M.A. Center and as the legal counsel for the ashram, was diagnosed in February 2007 with pancreatic cancer. Although the prognosis was not encouraging, Steve took the news in quite a positive manner, like so many other devotees who have been diagnosed with a terminal illness. He said that the situation was actually an opportunity for all his spiritual practices to finally bear fruit. Amma was very upset when she heard the news of her darling son's illness. She frequently discussed his diagnosis with other devotees. Likewise, Steve said that he was trying to keep Amma in his thoughts as much as possible. When our time comes to leave the body, the most important thing to do is to focus on Amma as much as possible since in reality she is the only one who will be there for us as we make our transition and continue our journey into the astral plane.

By the end of April, the cancer had spread throughout his body, and he bravely stopped chemotherapy. On April 28th, Amma called Steve from India. She was very upset, obviously feeling his pain as well as that of his wife, Marilyn, and daughter, Shakti. Swamiji, who was translating, said that Amma was crying so much that she could not speak.

Our beloved Amma surely gave peace to Steve as his soul made his final journey from the earthly plane to the astral world. Although Steve experienced much physical pain during the last few weeks of his life, he was blessed to be not only surrounded by loving family members and close devotee friends in a spiritually uplifting environment, but also to receive solace over the phone from Amma herself, the Divine Mother of the Universe.

Amma arranged the perfect time for Steve to pass away. The ashram residents were informed of his passing on May 3, 2007, about an hour after the evening program ended, so that the ashram residents were able to go to Steve's house to chant the *Sri Lalita Sahasranama*. How special that he left his body on Thursday, the day of the week dedicated to the Guru, at 10:08 p.m. (1008 being an auspicious number in Hinduism).

I have had a fear of death my entire life, ever since I saw a dead body as a child, and have always been afraid to be around death. However, when I entered Steve's house less than an hour after his passing, I was struck by the deep sense of peace I felt. Steve's wife, daughter, and sister greeted the ashram residents, and all the family members seemed to be in a meditative and tranquil state. I felt that Amma's presence had created such a peaceful environment.

When I entered the room and gazed at Steve's body, he looked peaceful, dressed in white, wearing his mala and covered in rose petals with an Amma doll curled up next to his body. Above him was a large, beautiful picture of Amma so that in his final days Steve could look upward at her beatific countenance, as Mother would lead him upward toward our divine home. I was told that before he passed, when the chant of *"Om Namah Shivayah"* was played, although he slipped in and out of consciousness, his hands instinctively went into a *mudra* (gesture formed by the hands and fingers that has a mystical significance) and stayed that way until his passing. As the ashram residents and his family sat around the body chanting the 1,000 names of the Divine Mother, I felt Amma's presence in the room giving peace and repose to all present, and I clearly felt Steve's soul above us. As I left the house, Marilyn calmly said, "He's in a better place."

As I meditated, sitting in front of Steve's body, I had a deep realization. He was no longer who I thought he was: an attorney with a wife and daughter, a homeowner, an energetic and frequently intense person. He was now simply a divine soul, which in essence is who he always was and always would be. Likewise, I contemplated the image of my own dead body, and realized that I'm not really who I thought I was. I've mistakenly identified with this temporary body. Then I visualized the lifeless bodies of my friends and family and realized that they are also falsely identified with their temporary existence, thinking they are the body, mind, and emotions; but none of that is who we truly are.

We are all essentially divine souls full of love and light. May we all increasingly feel and identify with Amma's divine light. May we become aware of her omniscient consciousness always surging within our short-lived bodies. In our remaining time on earth, through Amma's grace, may we exude compassion, forgiveness, detachment, and divine love toward all beings.

Om Amriteshwarayai Namah

Amma wrote the following inspiring words before she left the M.A. Center one summer many years ago:

Darling Children,

Amma sees all of you and remembers all of your work during Amma's visit here.

Amma is not far away from you. Amma is always with you. My children should learn to love this world. Start it from your house, and try to expand the love to society. First live a disciplined life. That is what Amma expects from all of you.

Love each other and forgive others' faults. God is love, so when you start loving others without expecting anything, it becomes a way to purify your mind. Our love should not be only for the satisfaction of the body, mind or intellect. It should be selfless.

Amma comes to you everyday and gives kisses to you all.

Affectionate kisses for Amma's darling children.

Om Namah Shivaya,

Amma

Glossary

Adharma: Unrighteous behavior; deviation from natural harmony.

Amrita: Divine nectar; the nectar of immortality.

Arati: Clockwise movement of a lamp aflame with burning camphor, to propitiate a deity, Guru, or venerated person, usually signifying the closing of a ceremonial worship.

Archana: Recitation of divine names.

Ashram: The home of a group of people who lead a spiritual life, generally the home of a spiritual teacher. "a"—"that" and "shramam"—"effort" (toward self-realization).

Ayurveda: The ancient healing system of India.

Bhagavad Gita: Literally, "Song of the Lord," it consists of 18 chapters of verses in which Lord Krishna advises Arjuna. The advice is given on the battlefield of Kurukshetra, just before the righteous Pandavs fight the unrighteous Kauravas. It is a practical guide to overcoming crises in one's personal or social life, and is the essence of Vedic wisdom.

Bhajan: Devotional song or hymn in praise of God.

Bhava: Divine mood or state.

Brahmachari: Celibate male disciple who practices spiritual disciplines under a Guru's guidance. (Brahmacharini is the female equivalent.)

Brahmasthanam temple: Born out of Amma's divine intuition, these unique temples are open to everyone irrespective of their religion. The central icon is four-sided, displaying Ganesha, Shiva, Devi, and the Serpent, emphasizing the inherent unity underlying the manifold aspects of the Divine. At present, there are 16 such temples throughout India and one in Mauritius.

Darshan: Audience with a holy person or vision of the divine. In Amma's organization, this specifically refers to Amma's embrace.

Devi Bhava: "The Divine Mood of Devi," the state in which Amma reveals her oneness and identity with the Divine Mother.

Dharma: Literally, "that which upholds (creation)." Generally used to refer to the harmony of the universe, a righteous code of conduct, sacred duty, or eternal law.

Divine Mother: A manifestation of God in the feminine form.

Ganesha: The elephant-headed Hindu deity, who is the son of Shiva and Parvati; known as the remover of obstacles.

Guru: One who removes the darkness of ignorance; spiritual master/ guide.

Guru Purnima: Literally, "full moon of the Guru." It commemorates the birthday of Veda Vyasa, the illustrious compiler of the Vedas and other scriptures.

Japa: Repeating a mantra.

Ji: A suffix denoting respect.

Jiva: Individual soul.

Kali: Goddess associated with *shakti* (empowerment). The word "kali" comes from "kala," which means "time" or "black" ("dark-colored"). In association with time, Kali is the goddess of time (or change, and by extension, death). In association with "black," Kali is one who was even before light came into existence, and is therefore beyond time. Also, the consort of Shiva.

Karma: Action; mental, verbal, and physical activity.

Krishna: Principal incarnation of Lord Vishnu. He was born in a royal family but was raised by foster parents, and lived as a cowherd boy in Vrindavan, where He was loved and worshipped by his devoted companions, the *gopis* (milkmaids) and *gopas* (cowherds). Krishna later established the city of Dwaraka. He was a friend and adviser to his cousins, the Pandavas, especially Arjuna, whom He served as charioteer during the Mahabharata War, and to whom He revealed His teachings as the Bhagavad Gita.

Krishna Bhava: "The Divine Mood of Krishna," the state in which Amma reveals her oneness and identity with Lord Krishna.

Kurukshetra: Battlefield on which the Pandavas and Kauravas fought the Mahabharata War, and where Krishna dispensed to Arjuna spiritual advice that forms the Bhagavad Gita.

Leela: Divine play.

Loka: World.

Mahatma: Great soul.

Mantra: A sound, syllable, word or words of spiritual content. Originally, a revelation of *rishis* (seers) that arose during deep contemplation.

Mata: Mother

Mata Amritanandamayi: "Mother of Immortal Bliss" (Mother's full name is Sri Mata Amritanandamayi Devi).

Maya: Cosmic delusion, personified as a temptress. Illusion; appearance, as contrasted with Reality; the creative power of the Lord.

Moksha: Liberation from the realm of births and deaths.

Mudra: Gesture formed by the hands and fingers having a mystical significance.

Peetham: Platform/seat for the Guru.

Pitta: Fire constitution in Ayurveda.

Prarabdha: The fruits of actions from previous lives that one is destined to experience in the present life.

Pranam: To bow down with folded hands.

Prasad: Sacred offering, usually food blessed by the Guru.

Puja: Ritualistic or ceremonial worship.

Realization (often prefixed with "Self-" or "God-"): The state of complete identity with God.

Sadhak: A spiritual seeker.

Sadhana: Spiritual practices.

Samadhi: Blissful state of absorption in God.

Samsara: Cycle of births and deaths.

Sanatana Dharma: The Eternal Truth/Principle; original name for Hinduism.

Sankalpa: Divine Resolve.

Sannyasi: A monk who has taken formal vows of renunciation (*sanyasa*); traditionally wears an ocher-colored robe, representing the burning away of all desires.

Satguru: Literally, "true master." One who, while still experiencing the bliss of the Self, chooses to come down to the level of ordinary people in order to help them grow spiritually.

Satsang: Being in communion with the Supreme Truth. Also, being in the company of the Mahatmas, studying scriptures, listening to a spiritual talk or discussion, and participating in spiritual practices in a group setting.

Self: Atman, the eternal self: God; one's spiritual essence, not identified with body or mind.

Seva: Selfless service.

Sevak: A devotee performing selfless service.

Shiva: The Auspicious One; the masculine principle; the aspect of the Trinity associated with the dissolution of the universe.

Shraddha: Awareness, faith.

Siddha: Someone with occult powers.

Tapas: Spiritual austerities.

Vasanas: Latent tendencies or subtle desires of the mind resulting from prior actions, and which manifest as thought and action.

Vata: Air constitution in Ayurveda.

Vedas: Most ancient of all scriptures, originating from God, the Vedas were not composed by any human author but were "revealed" in deep meditation to the ancient rishis. These sagely revelations came to be known as Vedas, of which there are four: *Rig, Yajus, Sama* and *Atharva*).

References

Amritaswarupananda, Swami, *Awaken Children, Volumes I—VII; Dialogues with Mata Amritanandamayi*, San Ramon, CA: M.A. Center, 1995.

Ramakrishnananda, Swami, *The Secret of Inner Peace*, San Ramon, CA: M.A. Center, 2006.

Sri Mata Amritanandamayi Devi, *The Eternal Truth*, Kerala, India; Mata Amritanandamayi Mission Trust, 2006.

Zeff, Ted (Dayalu), *Searching For God, Part I*, San Ramon, CA: Shiva Publishing, 1997.

Zeff, Ted (Dayalu), *Searching For God, Part II*, San Ramon, CA: Shiva Publishing, 2002.

Resources

For information about Amma's tours, satsang groups throughout the world, books, and visiting her ashrams, please visit: www.amma.org or www.amritapuri.org

CPSIA information can be obtained
at www.ICGtesting.com
Printed in the USA
BVOW10s2157240516

R7057100001B/R70571PG448964BVX1B/1/P